Scotland's Roman Remains

An Introduction and Handbook

LAWRENCE KEPPIE

Curator (Archaeology), Hunterian Museum
University of Glasgow

Foreword
EDWINA V. W. PROUDFOOT

JOHN DONALD PUBLISHERS LTD
EDINBURGH

ISBN 0 85976 157 6

Exclusive distribution in the United States of America and Canada by Humanities Press Inc., Atlantic Highlands, NJ 07716, USA

Filmset by J&L Composition, Filey, North Yorkshire
Printed in Great Britain by Bell & Bain Ltd., Glasgow

Foreword

As an outpost of empire, Scotland played a significant, if unusual, role in the Roman world. The south and east were occupied intermittently from 79 AD to the early third century, while the north and west remained outside Roman control, though certainly not beyond influence. The conquest was therefore incomplete in Scotland, and military occupation was not followed up by a period of peaceful development, during which the natives would have been Romanised, with consequent political changes. No towns were built in Scotland, where remains are of camps and forts for the most part. If any villas were built, none has been discovered.

Nevertheless the Romans left an important imprint on Scotland. This is the first historic period, with documentary evidence of the occupation, some of which also sheds light on the natives. In addition archaeological research has led to detailed understanding of the range and distribution of the forts and other sites, while recently through aerial photography a considerable number of discoveries have been made, some filling gaps in knowledge and others opening up new avenues of enquiry. Excavation of many forts and camps has allowed a closer study of specific sites, clarifying details both locally and throughout the occupied zone in Scotland.

Much of this information is held in museums and in publications, but it is true to say that Scotland's Roman remains are not well known or well understood in Scotland or elsewhere, except in academic circles, where they form an integral part of frontier studies.

When the Council for British Archaeology Scotland approached Lawrence Keppie to write *Scotland's Roman Remains*, he was asked to explain the importance of the remains for Scotland and set them in context, a different approach from usual. Emphasis has been placed on sites in their setting and on reasons for their location as well as on the visible remains and their interpretation.

Lawrence Keppie is a Roman scholar with unrivalled knowledge of many aspects of Roman archaeology. In *Scotland's Roman Remains* he has written an exciting account of the monuments of the Roman occupation, interpreting these skilfully with diagrams, site plans and many photographs. He also discusses excavated artefacts, explaining these in their Roman context, and indicating where they may be seen. The book is written in an engaging, flowing style that is easy to read, but which nevertheless provides considerable detail. In particular the gazetteer will be useful to visitors who want to know what they will actually see when they visit a particular site, as well as how each monument fits into the history of the Romans in Scotland.

This is the second collaborative text commissioned by the Council for British Archaeology Scotland, and others are planned. Lawrence Keppie and John Donald have co-operated on this occasion to produce a book that CBA Scotland feels will fill a gap in the general literature and will appeal to many readers whom we hope will feel encouraged to visit these sites from Scotland's Roman past.

Edwina V. W. Proudfoot, President

The Council for British Archaeology Scotland is a voluntary organisation. Its wide membership is interested in protecting and promoting the archaeological remains of Scotland's past, through publications and other means, especially by working with other bodies. Its address is: CBA Scotland, Royal Museum of Scotland, 1 Queen Street, Edinburgh EH2 1JD.

Acknowledgements

This handbook was commissioned by the Council for British Archaeology Scotland, and I am grateful to Edwina Proudfoot, currently president of CBAS, for inviting me in the first instance to write it. I am grateful also to James Walker and Margaret Robb who shared with me the pleasure and effort of locating and visiting most of the sites described below, and of looking at them with fresh eyes; to the Hunterian Museum of the University of Glasgow for financial help towards visiting some of the more distant sites; to Dr. D. J. Breeze who read the complete text in typescript, and Gordon Maxwell who read Part II (the 'itineraries'). I was delighted to be able to draw upon their extensive knowledge of individual sites. Both made many useful suggestions for improvement, which were gratefully incorporated. I am also grateful to the staffs of museums throughout Scotland who replied to a questionnaire regarding their displays and answered detailed enquiries. In particular I have to thank Trevor Cowie of the Royal Museum of Scotland (formerly the National Museum of Antiquities), Geoff Bailey and David Devereux of Falkirk Museum, Andrew Gibb and Bill Hanson of Glasgow University, Guthrie Hutton of BBC Scotland, and Susan Bryson, for advice on specific points. Alan Wishart assisted in the checking of bibliographical details and Elizabeth Tough checked National Grid References for sites mentioned in the text.

Prof. J. J. Wilkes kindly provided an up-to-date plan of Carpow, and Nicholas Holmes a plan of his and earlier work at Cramond. Prof. S. S. Frere made available plans of Inchtuthil in advance of publication. Fig. 10 was drawn by Duncan Campbell after an original by Maggie Wallace. The other line illustrations were drawn by the author; those which he redrew from published sources are acknowledged in the text.

Permission to reproduce photographs was given by the Ministry of Defence, BBC Scotland, the Committee for Aerial Photography (University of Cambridge), the Royal Commission on the Ancient and Historical Monuments of Scotland, the Hunterian Museum of the University of Glasgow (and the Hunter Coin Cabinet), the Royal

Museum of Scotland, and Falkirk Museum. Dr. A. A. R. Henderson, Sandy Sharp and Colin Martin generously allowed me to use photographs from their own collections. I am particularly grateful to Trevor Graham and his colleagues of the Photographic Unit, University of Glasgow, for their help in preparing many of the photographs for publication.

The present guide stands in a long tradition: readers may recall the two monographs by Jessie Mothersole (*Agricola's Road into Scotland* and *In Roman Scotland*, both published in 1927), delightfully illustrated by her own sketches and watercolours. In 1960 Professor Anne Robertson's excellent handbook to *The Antonine Wall* was published by the Glasgow Archaeological Society, and has been several times reprinted and revised. More recently Dr. David Breeze published his booklet *Roman Scotland: a Guide to the Visible Remains* (Newcastle 1979). The present handbook has benefited from a more generous word-allowance and the opportunity for extensive illustration.

The Hunterian Museum now houses a Roman Scotland Archive, the compilation of which, based on copies of Ordnance Survey record cards of Roman sites, was made possible under a scheme financed by the Manpower Services Commission; I am grateful to Derek Maguire, Catriona Martin and Morag Cross who assisted in its compilation. The existence of the Archive proved an invaluable aid towards the preparation of the 'itineraries' and of the Bibliography.

Finally I must offer a word of thanks to John Tuckwell for accepting the manuscript so readily for publication and seeing it rapidly through to a finished product.

Lawrence Keppie, Glasgow.

Contents

Introduction

When the Romans first came to Britain in AD 43, in the reign of the emperor Claudius, it may be doubted whether they had any clear intention of advancing as far north as Scotland. However, early successes in overrunning southern England drew Roman armies forwards first into northern England and then, in the years after AD 79, into Scotland.

The Romans remained in Scotland, on and off, for at least a century and a half, and exercised some considerable influence over events there for much longer. Yet today it is a commonly held belief that Hadrian's Wall, that stupendous monument to Roman power on the crags between Tyne and Solway, was the northern limit to the Roman domain in Britain. This view is widely held both in Scotland – where it testifies to the unconquerable spirit of the native peoples against an invader – and in England where everything north of Hadrian's Wall is considered beyond the Roman pale.

Scotland can boast of no Roman towns or villas, so frequent in areas further to the South. In general the archaeological remains to be discussed here are the remnants of the military installations of a great Empire, built more often in timber and turf than in mortared stonework.

The following pages also contain a brief description of the categories of small finds – inscribed stones and altars, coins, brooches, even cooking pots, shoes and belt buckles – which were lost, left behind or broken by the army of occupation, and serve to provide us with a fascinating picture of life in the frontier area of Rome's northernmost province.

The handbook is designed to appeal to the reader with little or no prior knowledge of things Roman, yet who wishes to learn something about a brief but action-packed interlude in Scotland's past, when the northern part of the island of Britain became a part of the Roman Empire. It aims also to provide an impression of how our picture of the Roman period is built up from the literary accounts and the archaeological evidence, so that the reader may see what can be legitimately inferred and what must remain, inevitably, hidden from the modern enquirer.

If this handbook achieves anything, it will be to encourage the reader to go out and locate the remains for himself, and visualise their appearance nearly 2000 years ago. The itineraries (below, pp. 71–170) aim to provide an indication of what may be seen at individual sites, against the backcloth of Scotland's spectacular scenery. There is the further hope that this guidebook will help the reader to be able to *recognise* sites as being Roman, to perceive what distinguishes them from monuments of earlier or more recent epochs, even where no archaeological excavation has ever taken place.

In the following pages two liberties are taken with the name Scotland: firstly that it is used at all, when the reader will remember that the Scots from whom the northern half of the island of Britain takes its present name had not yet migrated across the Irish Channel; secondly that the term will be employed on occasion to encompass all the territory between Shetland and the river Tyne – that is, Scotland can be everything north of Carlisle and Newcastle, and so includes great parts of present-day Northumbria and a little of Cumbria. The Romans knew of no Anglo-Scottish Border on the present line; whenever they moved northwards, their starting point was the Tyne-Solway isthmus.

Key to the Maps

■   fort
■   fortlet
●   watch-tower
□   camp
— · —   road (course certain)
— — —   road (course probable)
_ / _   milestone
Land over 250 m (800 ft) stippled
Note: the abbreviation RCAHMS = Royal Commission on the Ancient and Historical Monuments of Scotland.

Part 1

The Romans in Scotland

CHAPTER 1

Scotland on the Eve of the Roman Invasion

It has been prevalent in some circles to suppose that when the Romans arrived in Scotland, no-one else lived there, or that everyone else promptly left. In fact Scotland had been occupied by man for over 6000 years since the retreat of the ice sheets had drawn hunters and fishermen to eke out a scanty living in these northern climes. By the mid-1st century AD the tribes of Scotland were making use of iron

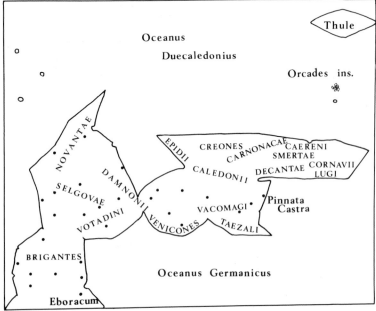

1. **Ptolemy's Map**, compiled c. AD 140, showing the major tribes. Much of the information about the interior of Scotland must derive from data collected by Agricola's army in AD 79–83. It is not known why Scotland 'leans over' to the east. Note: The *Orcades Insulae* are the Orkneys; *Thule* is Shetland (or perhaps Iceland). Dots represent places individually named by Ptolemy. *Eboracum* = York. *Pinnata Castra* is a site somewhere on the Moray Firth (see also p. 00).

tools and weapons, and had long since begun the sowing and harvesting of crops. In Scotland this so-called Iron Age and the Roman period are contemporary – or more precisely the Roman invasions amounted to a mere interlude (or even a hiccup) in the Scottish Iron Age.

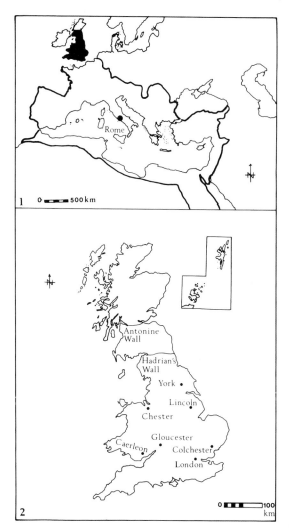

2. Above: **The Roman Empire**, c. AD 140, during the reign of Antoninus Pius. Below: **Roman Britain**, c. AD 140, showing some of the chief towns and the two frontier walls.

Scotland was not a unified country at this time, but was divided into territories owing allegiance to individual tribes. The geographer Ptolemy, who compiled a world map about AD 140, provides a useful picture of the tribes and the areas they controlled (Fig. 1). The Novantae occupied south-west Scotland, the Selgovae held an upland area further east centred on the upper valley of the Tweed, and the Votadini controlled a wide area of the Lothians between the Forth and the Tweed. The Damnonii belonged in Ayrshire and the central Lowlands. Beyond them were the Venicones of Fife, the Vacomagi round the coastline of NE Scotland, and numerous smaller tribes. For the Romans all the land north of the Forth–Clyde line was known as Caledonia, a zone of mountains and trackless forests inhabited by wild naked savages untouched by civilisation.

Essentially this was a warrior society of Celtic peoples, owing allegiance to local chieftains. Archeology shows a wide variety of settlement-types in use in Scotland: circular stone-built or timber houses in central and southern Scotland, together with crannogs (lochside hutments often raised out of the water on wooden piles), souterrains (underground stores associated with circular huts at ground level), duns (low circular stone towers), and brochs (lofty stone towers). There were no towns. As centres of population, or at least centres of defence, we can see the hillforts which abound in most areas, though a great many were probably long abandoned when the Romans came.

CHAPTER 2

The Romans in Scotland: an Historical Outline

The Romans first came to Britain in 55 BC when Julius Caesar and his legions landed on a beach near Dover. Caesar's exploits in Britain in 55 (and in greater strength in 54) were short-lived, even though he claimed the total subjection of Britain to impress public opinion at Rome. Almost exactly a century later, the emperor Claudius mounted a full-scale invasion of Britain, and his forces quickly overran the south-eastern corner of the island. Progress thereafter was slow, and the province was all but lost to Rome in AD 60–61 with the outbreak of a major rebellion under Boudica – the Boadicea of legend. A civil war in AD 68–69 brought to power a new dynasty, the Flavians, who initiated a forward movement in Britain: northern England and Wales were overrun, and the way was cleared for a major assault on the northern half of the island. The governor chosen to lead the Roman armies into Scotland was Gnaeus Julius Agricola, a safe and uninspiring supporter of the Flavian dynasty, who had twice before seen service in Britain.

Agricola's campaigns

Our appreciation of Agricola's activities is immeasurably enriched by the survival to modern times of an account of his life written a few years later by his son-in-law, the distinguished historian Cornelius Tacitus. This matrimonial connection effectively secured Agricola's posthumous fame, and has given us a detailed account of and chronological framework for his campaigns in northern Britain. Without it we should not know exactly when the Romans first penetrated into Scotland, how many seasons the army campaigned there, and what the outcome was.

Agricola arrived in Britain as governor in the late summer of AD 77 (the date now preferred by most scholars; the alternative is AD 78) and undertook a lightning campaign in North Wales, to put an end to

7

resistance there. In the following year he consolidated Roman control over northern England. By the early summer of AD 79 he was ready to move further north. Assembling a substantial battle-group which must have numbered some 20,000 men (based on the four legions available, together with auxiliary troops; see below, p. 21), he advanced through southern Scotland to the line of the Forth and then to the Tay. Tacitus does not report any resistance from the tribes, but notes that bad weather hindered the army's advance. In the following year (80, which Agricola could reasonably have supposed would be his last in Britain – governors normally served for about three years on a single posting), he concentrated his efforts on consolidation work within areas already overrun and on the placing of garrisons along the outer limits of the newly enlarged province. In particular he established forts in the valley between Forth and Clyde, which he saw would make a suitable northern frontier line. However, in Rome it seems likely that the emperor Titus was sufficiently impressed by the ease of Agricola's advance to extend his appointment (probably for a further three-year period), with instructions to continue. How far the emperor appreciated the nature of the terrain that Agricola's army would now have to face is unknown to us.

In the spring of AD 81 Agricola turned again to his task. He placed garrisons on the coast facing Ireland and allegedly pondered an expedition there. More important, he began an investigation of land routes up the west coast, taking part in at least one sea-crossing, perhaps into Argyllshire. In the same summer he despatched some ships up the west coast.

One summer was enough to show Agricola that the best way northwards in Britain was not up the west coast, with its almost continuous belts of mountains and sea lochs. In AD 82 he turned his attention to the east coast and moved forward from the Tay into Strathmore, on the traditional route followed by invaders from the south. But the tribes proved an elusive quarry, adept all the while at falling upon his extended communication lines, and he suffered a setback when the Caledonians assaulted one of his task-forces, and they were beaten off only with some difficulty.

In the following year (AD 83) events moved towards a climax. Agricola must have known that his own term of office could not be much more prolonged; equally the emperor in Rome, Domitian (who succeeded Titus in September AD 81), with his mind on campaigns in Germany, may well have encouraged Agricola to bring the British war

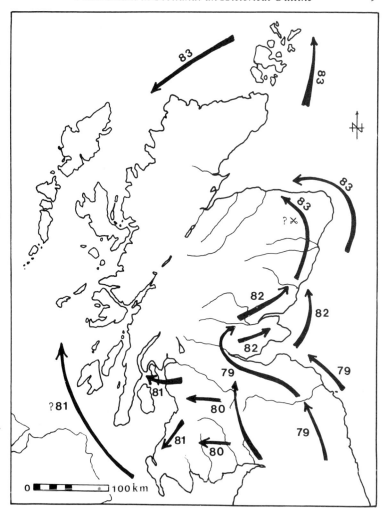

3. **Agricola's campaigns by land and sea, AD 79–83**, which culminated in a battle at *Mons Graupius*.

to a prompt and suitable close, with fanfares to indicate an acceptable victory. Tacitus tells us nothing about the movements of Agricola's forces in the spring and early summer of AD 83. We may assume that no engagement was fought; certainly none was won. As to the whereabouts of the army, archaeology indicates that in AD 82 or 83 (or in the course of both summers) Agricola had succeeded in moving forward past the Grampian mountains into the flatter country of Moray and Nairn, where he is known to have reached the valley of the Spey and may easily have gone further.

By the late summer of 83, with the Caledonians as elusive as ever, and Agricola's own time running out, word came of a concentration of Caledonian warriors, some 30,000 in all, under a war-leader, Calgacus, at a hill which Tacitus names as *Mons Graupius* (the Graupian Mountain). Agricola advanced quickly to this position, with a minimum of heavy baggage, to confront the tribesmen before they repented of a decision to face the Romans in a set-piece encounter.

Agricola formed up his army in traditional Roman fashion, with auxiliary infantry in the centre and cavalry on each flank. But he held back his main strength, the legions, as a reserve, and in the event they were not needed. The Caledonians had a large number of war-chariots (a military vehicle long relegated on the Continent to museums and ceremonial parades); Roman cavalry soon dispersed them. The auxiliaries then advanced up the slope of *Mons Graupius* and, just as they seemed likely to be enveloped by the masses of Caledonians filtering round their flanks down the hillside, Agricola unleashed a reserve force of 2000 cavalry in flank and rear; victory was his. Tacitus gives Roman casualties at 360 and Caledonian losses at about 10,000. After

4. **Mount Bennachie**, perhaps the battle-site of *Mons Graupius*, seen from the marching camp at Durno. (Photo: Dr. A. A. R. Henderson.) See also p. 168.

the battle Agricola instructed his fleet to sail round the north coast of Scotland, from east to west, as though to emphasise the totality of the conquest.

The location of *Mons Graupius* has never been satisfactorily established. Tacitus implies that it lay close to, and perhaps even within sight of, the sea, and far away in the very north of Britain. A good case has been made out in recent years for identifying *Mons Graupius* with the great mass of Bennachie close to Inverurie, near which a large Roman marching camp was located by aerial photography at Durno in the later 1970s (below, p. 168). A mistake in the text of Tacitus' biography of Agricola, when it was set as a printed book in the 1470s, led to the spelling *Grampius* instead of *Graupius*; hence our Grampian Mountains, and more recently Grampian Television and Grampian Region, all of which should be 'Graupian'!

The battle at *Mons Graupius* formed the climax to Agricola's governorship, and shortly afterwards (with the end of the campaigning season) he was recalled to Rome, and never again commanded an army in the field. Agricola's successor, whose name remains unknown, saw to the establishment of many forts and roads in Scotland, deep into Strathmore. The kingpin of the system was a fortress for a legion, of some 53 acres (21.5 ha.), at Inchtuthil on the Tay (below, p. 160). Construction work there was underway in AD 86. Forts were also placed at the mouths of glens leading in towards the Highlands, and others on lines of communication back to the Tay, the Forth and the southern part of the British province.

With the departure of Agricola a veil is drawn over the history of Scotland for half a century. The modern historian is abruptly thrown back on the archaeological record whose imperfections become all too apparent. The years following AD 85 witnessed a sequence of Roman disasters in her Balkan provinces, involving a serious loss of troops, and the garrison of Britain was cut back to fill the gaps. The opportunity was thus lost, if it had ever existed, of completing for Rome the conquest of the entire island. The base at Inchtuthil was abandoned in about 87 and with it all the forts north of the Tay. The Roman army fell back to the line of the river Earn. Within a few years a further withdrawal had begun, which brought Roman troops back to the Forth–Clyde line, and very shortly to the Cheviots. The archaeological record is insufficiently precise to allow every stage in the withdrawal to be documented. However, by the turn of the century it seems clear that the Roman forces had fallen back to the Tyne–Solway

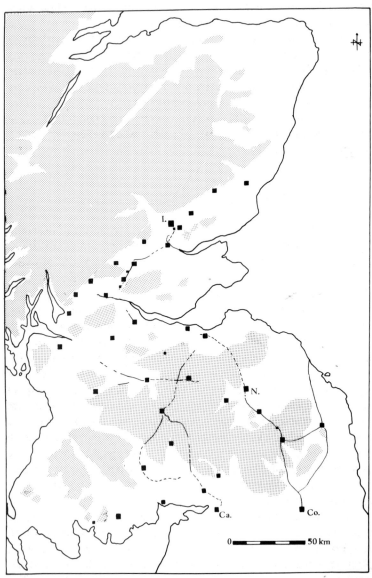

5. Forts and roads in Scotland in the Flavian period, AD 83–c. 100 (after Breeze). Note: Ca. = Carlisle, Co. = Corbridge, I. = Inchtuthil, N. = Newstead.

line, along which a cordon of military posts was subsequently established. When in the early 120s AD, under the emperor Hadrian, a great barrier of stone and turf – Hadrian's Wall – was built along the crags just north of this line, it must have seemed that the Roman interlude in Scotland's past was decisively over.

The departure of the Roman garrisons from Scotland left something of a power vacuum – a vacuum which it seems possible was filled by the arrival in central Scotland of broch-building tribesmen from the north, whose distinctive circular towers have been found in the Forth valley, in the Lothians and in the Tweed valley, with some evidence of construction and use at this time.

The Antonine period

In AD 138 Hadrian was succeeded by the man we know as Antoninus Pius. His accession had an immediate effect on the frontier in Britain. The army was ordered to move forward again and to begin construction of a new frontier line, this time in central Scotland – the Antonine Wall. A biography of Antoninus, written nearly two centuries later, reports that Antoninus 'having thrust back the barbarians and having built a second wall, this time of turf, conquered the Britons through his legate Lollius Urbicus'. This new wall (Britain already had one wall – Hadrian's) was built in AD 142–143; coins were issued to mark the successful northwards extension of the British province. We may think that the decision to move forward again was testimony to disturbances and unrest in northern Britain, and even of the failure of the newly completed Hadrian's Wall. More probably, however, the advance has to be linked to Antoninus' need – like that of Claudius a century before – to acquire some military prestige; his advisers may have felt that it could be most easily won in Britain, by what in effect was a recovery of lands already overrun and briefly held at the time of Agricola's campaigns half a century before.

The Antonine Wall, built of turf on a substantial base of sandstone boulders, stretched for 37 miles (60 km) between Bo'ness on the Forth and Old Kilpatrick on the Clyde (below, p. 114). Along the line of the Wall were placed fortlets, very probably at every mile, and at wider intervals there were forts each housing a regiment of auxiliaries. The building of the Wall was commemorated by the setting up along its line of large stone plaques – known as distance slabs – inscribed with

6. **Defeat of the native tribes AD 142–43**, a scene from the sculptured distance slab found in 1868 at Bridgeness, West Lothian. (Photo: National Museums of Scotland.)

Latin texts giving details of the distances completed by each work-party (below, p. 46). The task was undertaken by men from the three legions of the garrison of Britain. After a year or so, extra forts were added, at much closer intervals.

The Antonine Wall did not exist in isolation. Many forts were built along the main communication routes in southern Scotland, often on

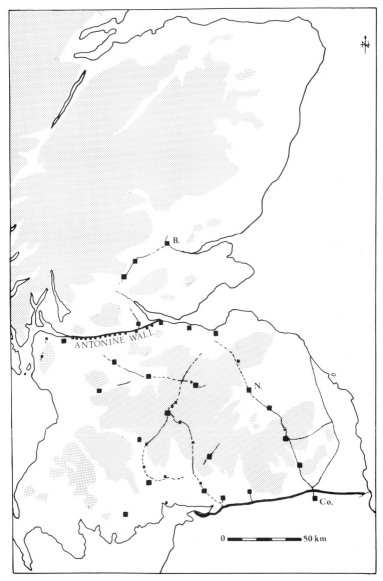

7. Forts and roads in Scotland in the Antonine period, AD 142–c. AD 165 (after Breeze). Note: B. = Bertha, Co. = Corbridge, N. = Newstead.

sites used by Agricola's troops. A detailed record must have been kept from the time of the earlier occupation; doubtless ramparts and ditches would still be visible, if somewhat overgrown after the passage of half a century. A few forts were also constructed north of the Antonine Wall, as far as the mouth of the Tay. It may be that these were intended to close off, or protect, the peninsula of Fife, whose inhabitants (from the archaeological record a culturally distinct grouping) seem thus to have been afforded some protection by Rome.

Around AD 155/157 there was trouble on the northern frontier line. Many forts – perhaps the entire system – were abandoned; some were certainly burnt down, though whether by attacking tribesmen or departing garrisons is difficult to gauge. Within a year or two most of the forts had been rebuilt or refurbished. But soon after the accession in AD 161 of a new emperor, Marcus Aurelius (or at least within the decade 160–170), most of the forts in Scotland had been abandoned once more, this time for good. The army returned to the line of Hadrian's Wall, whose installations were refurbished to receive them. A few forts were maintained northwards into Dumfriesshire and as far as the Tweed until about 180, but by that date, or soon after, the garrisons were pulled back further, and Hadrian's Wall with some forward outposts to the Cheviots became effectively the northern frontier of the province.

The expedition of Severus

In general, although specific information is lacking, it seems that the northern frontier in Britain was restive throughout the decades following the Roman withdrawal from Scotland. Finally in AD 208 the emperor Septimius Severus arrived in Britain, with his sons Caracalla and Geta, together with substantial military forces, to mount a major campaign in the North, specifically against two tribes – named as the Maeatae (perhaps in Stirlingshire and Strathmore), and the Caledonians who lived 'beyond them'. In AD 209 the imperial task-force, perhaps some 40,000 men, crossed the line of Hadrian's Wall and (according to the historian Cassius Dio who wrote soon after) invaded 'Caledonia'. Very probably a fleet accompanied the army up the east coast. Casualties were heavy, but the advance continued until the emperor arrived 'almost at the end of the island'. A treaty was arranged with the native tribes, now suitably cowed,

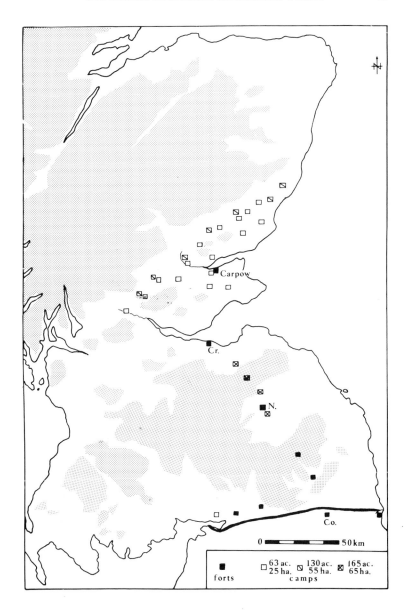

8. **Campaigns of the emperor Septimius Severus, AD 208–211**, showing marching camps north of Hadrian's Wall, and forts reoccupied at this time (after Breeze). Note: Co. = Corbridge, Cr. = Cramond, N. = Newstead.

by which some territory was yielded, and Severus took the title *Britannicus*, 'conqueror of Britain'. But the celebrations were premature: the next year was marked by a great rebellion which was suppressed, probably by Caracalla, as Severus himself was ill. One reason for revolt may have been the realisation that the Romans intended to remain in Scotland, for construction had very probably already begun on a fortress for about half a legion at Carpow on the southern side of the Tay at Newburgh; both the Second and the Sixth legions had a part in the building work (below, p.154). This was a new Inchtuthil – a powerful base close up against the known or likely source of future trouble. Early in 211 Severus, worn down by old age and the pressures of an energetic life, died at York. Caracalla succeeded him, with the army's support. The ancient historians tell us that Caracalla left immediately for the continent and Italy, to consolidate his political position, abandoning the Scottish conquests. However, an inscribed stone from Carpow (below, p.154) may testify to continued building activity within the new reign. But it was not long before the army finally withdrew.

Scotland after the Roman Withdrawal

After the departure of Caracalla silence descends on the northern frontier for about a century. This may by itself imply that the Severan campaigns had been a success: the northern tribes had taken a severe beating, or enough of a shock to keep the frontier quiet for several generations. But if Scotland as such was abandoned, some permanent forts were maintained to the north of Hadrian's Wall as far as the Cheviots, their garrisons being large all-purpose auxiliary units of mixed infantry and cavalry, which would have had the capacity to range widely, even up to the Forth–Clyde line.

Although the Roman interlude in Scottish history was now effectively over – that is, the attempts to place military forces north of the Cheviots was not repeated – the Romans doubtless continued to try to influence the tribes of the North, seeking alliances, supporting factions in tribal strife, or promising largesse in return for peaceful relations. Roman patrols, it has been suggested, might still have been seen along the main river valleys beyond the formal frontier line. But from about the 290s onwards the Roman province began to suffer devastating raids from the North, and also from Ireland and the continent. The Romans were increasingly on the defensive, no longer holding the initiative and dictating terms.

Foremost among the enemies of Roman Britain in the centuries which followed were the Picts (*Picti*) who are first mentioned by a Roman historian under the year 297. In 306 they were defeated by the emperor Constantius Chlorus somewhere in the northern half of Britain, perhaps to the north of Hadrian's Wall, though no secure evidence for his activities has yet been found in Scotland itself. Popular imagination supposes that the Picts were the chief adversaries of the Romans in earlier centuries too, but it seems that they had only become powerful towards the end of the 3rd century. Their origin has been much disputed, but the question need not concern us here. Most probably we should think of the name *Picti* (i.e. painted men) as implying a new power grouping in the North rather than indicating a tribe newly arrived from elsewhere. At any rate the weight and severity of their attacks on Roman Britain increased, and contributed substantially to the decline of the province's prosperity.

By the time the clouds partly lift to reveal the Scotland of the 7th century AD (occupied by Picts in the north and east, the Angles in the south-east, the British kingdom of Strathclyde and the incoming Scots on the west coast), the memory of a Roman occupation must have passed almost completely from the minds of the population, kept alive only in popular legend and by a few scholars until the rediscovery of Latin literature at the Renaissance.

CHAPTER 3

The Roman Army

The Roman imperial army was the force which overran Scotland and added its more southerly part to the Roman Empire. In a popular (but mistaken) modern view this army consisted of stocky Italians, somewhat darker-skinned than the local tribes. 'They must have found it cold in winter' is a common remark, usually expressed in mixed tones of sympathy and amusement. In truth the Roman army in Scotland contained but few Italians, and almost certainly none who came from Rome itself.

In the period of Rome's growth from small city-state to the foremost power in Italy, and then of the Mediterranean world, her soldiers had indeed been drawn from her own citizens, for whom the task of fighting on the state's behalf was felt both as a duty and a privilege. After the civil wars of the later 1st century BC, the first Roman emperor, Augustus, introduced reforms which made the army a lifetime's career and its members professional soldiers. Since Italians soon proved unwilling to tolerate the new conditions which required long service in distant provinces, Augustus and subsequent emperors turned increasingly to the manpower of the provinces themselves. The Roman army ceased to be an army of Romans, but an army defending Rome – a city that few of them can have visited or were likely to see during the long years of military service. This transition was still in progress when Agricola's legions reached Scotland, but by the reign of Antoninus Pius it can be judged complete. The army had become a cosmopolitan force which resembled in equipment, training, tactics and general appearance the force of centuries before, but in actuality the soldiers were loyal to the emperor who paid them, and to the good things that the Empire had brought to their homelands, not to the Senate and People of the Roman city. Just as in the Second World War the British Army contained many not born in Britain and with a few words of English at their disposal on enlistment, so the Roman legions opened their ranks to the tribesmen of the provinces, who were straightaway given

20

9. **Roman Legionaries**. Trajan's Column, Rome. (Photo: Hunterian Museum.)

Roman names and citizenship and once in uniform could hardly be distinguished from their comrades. Many Roman soldiers must have had only a smattering of Latin when they joined the ranks, to be augmented by the vocabulary of the barrack room and the parade ground.

The Roman army in Britain, which moved north to enter Scotland in the later first century, then again in the mid-second, and briefly again in the early third, consisted of two main elements: legionaries and auxiliaries. All were professional soldiers, who joined for 25 years and might be held longer.

The legions were the backbone of the Roman army. Each legion contained some 5000 legionaries, arranged into 10 cohorts of about 480 men; the cohorts themselves were divided into centuries of 80 men and into squads of eight, the basic unit (called a *contubernium*), who shared a tent while the army was on campaign and a barrack room in a permanent fortress. All the legionaries were armed and equipped alike as heavy infantry, with iron cuirasses, bronze or iron helmets, curving rectangular shields which offered substantial protection to the body, a short thrusting sword worn at the right side, and a dagger, as well as one or more throwing javelins. The legionaries were thus equipped both for attack and defence; needless to say they were generally expected to attack. The legion was commanded by its legate (*legatus legionis*) who held his post for about three years before moving

10. **Soldiers of the Roman army**. From top to bottom: auxiliary infantry-
man, auxiliary cavalryman, legionary. The soldiers are all wearing equipment
of the later 1st century AD. (Drawn by Duncan Campbell.)

on to another, probably civilian, appointment elsewhere in the Empire.

The legions were supported in battle by regiments of auxiliaries, who normally operated in front of the legions on a frontier line, while the latter constituted a strategic reserve. The auxiliaries were organised into cohorts (*cohortes*) of infantry usually of 480 men (on the legionary model – though some regiments were larger, up to 1000 men), and into *alae* (wings) of cavalry, usually about 500 men, though here too some regiments were of a larger size. Sometimes infantry and cavalry were combined in a single regiment, a *cohors equitata*, to increase its mobility and capability. These auxiliaries were non-citizens and would obtain citizenship on completion of their service, 25 years. The regiments took their names from the tribe or city of origin, for example the Sixth Cohort of Nervii (from the Low Countries), the First Cohort of Hamii, from the town of Hama in Syria, and the Second Cohort of Thracians (from Bulgaria), all of which were based for a time on the Antonine Wall in central Scotland.

In his biography of Agricola, Tacitus records that a newly enrolled cohort of Usipi (a tribe from the east bank of the Rhine near Frankfurt), formed about 80–82 and immediately transferred to Britain for training, where discipline was beaten into them by unsympathetic centurions, was roused to mutiny in the winter of 82/83 and killed its centurions. Commandeering three small vessels, the unhappy soldiers sailed for home round the north-west coast of Scotland; but few were to survive the hazards of hunger, cannibalism and stormy weather to reach the northern coast of Germany, where the survivors were promptly enslaved by local tribes unsympathetic to their plight. For a time after initial formation of auxiliary regiments, an attempt was made to keep up recruitment from the original source, but gradually the ranks of each regiment were filled from whatever manpower was available, usually from local sources within the province where the regiment was stationed. Though the regiments lost their particular ethnic nature, yet the traditions of the homeland, religious beliefs and any distinctive equipment might be retained, especially where regimental tradition required it. (So in the Second World War a few Englishmen wore the kilt of a Highland regiment!)

Men from Britain joined the Roman army: already at *Mons Graupius*

Agricola had among his army auxiliary regiments recruited in southern Britain. Regiments of auxiliaries were recruited in Britain, including probably southern Scotland after the conquest, and sent to other provinces: we happen to know of a man from Leicester who enlisted about AD 85 and shared in a moment of glory when his cohort of Britons were decorated in the field, and given citizenship 'before the completion of their due service' by the emperor Trajan during his great war in Dacia (modern Romania) in AD 106.

Agricola's army in the far north of Britain consisted of four legions: II *Augusta* ('Augustan'), II *Adiutrix* ('Supportive'), IX *Hispana* ('Spanish') and the XX *Valeria Victrix* ('Valiant and Victorious'). Soon after the end of Agricola's campaigns in the north, II *Adiutrix* was moved from Britain to the Danube frontier, to reinforce the garrisons there against serious inroads from across the river. Sometime in the period 110–120 legion IX *Hispana* was transferred to Germany, and then (it may be) to the eastern provinces of the Empire. Old theories about the 'disappearance' of the Ninth Legion, and the loss of its eagle-standard, in battle or by desertion in northern Britain, perhaps even in Scotland, have no foundation in the historical record and are now discredited. In about 122 legion VI *Victrix* ('Victorious') arrived in Britain from the Rhineland as a replacement. Thereafter the three legions, II *Augusta*, VI *Victrix* and XX *Valeria Victrix*, formed the permanent legionary garrison of Britain until the later fourth century.

As the army in Britain settled to a routine existence of patrols, manoeuvres and minor skirmishes, in the role of a frontier police, garrisons became more static; a soldier and his regiment might spend 25 years on a single posting. For men below the rank of centurion there was no system of transfers between provinces, to provide a variety of experience, terrain, climate and enemy. A posting to a legion or an auxiliary regiment stationed in Britain probably meant a lifetime in the island. For the garrison of a fort in northern Britain, the centre of the Empire and the city of Rome must have seemed very distant indeed.

CHAPTER 4

Roman Military Installations

What we see on the ground today in Scotland, or can observe from the air, are the camps, forts, roads and frontier works of the Roman army in what must often have been a hostile countryside. To the native tribes, the installations and the institutions of the armed forces of the Roman Empire must surely have been the cause of amazement and much interested observation. The neat square encampments, the trumpet calls, the religious ceremonies, the orderliness and the discipline have impressed countless observers down to modern times.

The military installations of the Roman army comprised temporary or 'marching' camps, forts, fortlets, watch-towers, the fortresses of the legions, and the roads which allowed prompt communication and swift reinforcement of the scattered garrisons. It is time now to consider each category in greater detail.

Temporary camps

Early editions of Ordnance Survey maps designated as Roman camps many upstanding earthworks of diverse period and size, which local pride over the years had ascribed to the Romans, even to Julius Caesar himself, in areas of Britain he cannot conceivably have traversed. Similarly in France *camps de César* proliferate. Sites which we can now see belong in the Iron Age, or which can be identified as mediaeval, were once happily designated Roman.

In the pages that follow, the term 'camp' is used for a temporary enclosure, used perhaps only once by a Roman army on the march, and defended by a single narrow ditch and a low mound. A 'fort', on the other hand, is a permanent base in use over many years, and containing timber or stone-built accommodation, where a soldier might spend a considerable part of his military service.

Delimiting an encampment serves to define it, and to discourage straying, and the unannounced or unwelcome arrival in the tent-lines

11. Legionaries engaged in the building of a camp. Trajan's Column, Rome. (Photo: Hunterian Museum.)

12. Tools for ditch-digging and wood-cutting. (Photo: Hunterian Museum.)

of two or four-legged intruders by night or day. Gradually the Roman camp-layout became standardised, if not fossilised, over the centuries. 'They seem,' says the military writer Vegetius, 'to carry a fortified city with them wherever they go.' The end product, certainly, was the throwing up in a brief space of two or three hours of a defended encampment within which each squad of men knew from long training the allotted position where their tent would be pitched.

Camps found in Scotland either by fieldwork or aerial reconnaissance have confirmed that the traditional layout was maintained. Camp defences consisted of a single ditch, usually v-shaped, with the spoil piled on the inner side to form a low rampart topped by palisade-stakes, of which each soldier carried two as part of his kit. Within the camp were lines of tents. In the centre of the camp were the larger tents of the commander and his staff.

Excavation of the interior of a camp normally reveals little to the archaeologist – at most some cooking areas or ovens, or refuse pits. In exceptional conditions the general layout of the tents within the camp may be reconstructed – aerial photographs of camps beside the legionary fortress at Inchtuthil show neat lines of refuse pits presumably next to each row of tents. Wooden tent-pegs, strikingly similar to the modern equivalent, have been recovered from several sites. The tents themselves were of leather, not canvas. Square or rectangular panels from Roman tents, preserved in damp conditions, have come from several sites in Scotland.

In Scotland many camps have survived as upstanding monuments in rough heathland, better perhaps than in any other part of the Roman Empire. They formed a source of great excitement to the surveyor William Roy when first he had them planned in the 1750s (below, p.58). Many can still be seen, though in a reduced state, even today. What visitor on the moors above Ardoch cannot be thrilled by the banks and ditches in the heather-covered landscape, as though abandoned by the Romans scarcely months ago? Other camps have been discovered only from the air (below, p.61), their ditches visible in the heat of a summer's drought as a green strip in a field under crop.

There is a great variation in size, between camps for small detachments and those housing large armies. Often camps of similar size are found at intervals of about 15–16 miles (24–26 km), the regular norm for a day's march. Some of those camps which lie in the vicinity of permanent forts may have served to house the fort-builders themselves. More often they must indicate only a task-force in transit

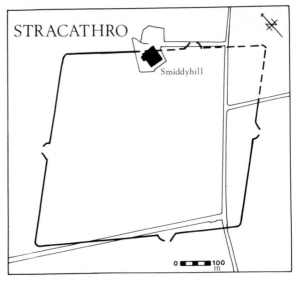

13. Stracathro, Angus: ground-plan of a marching camp with distinctive gateways, which can be dated to the Flavian period (after St. Joseph). See also Fig. 88.

which had stopped close to a fort. Small camps in the vicinity of the Antonine Wall are likely to have housed work-details engaged on the construction or maintenance of the frontier.

Because of the absence of interior buildings and the shortness of their lifespan, few small finds are made during the excavation of a camp. As a result camps may be difficult, or impossible, to date, unless a study of their size, relative proportions or some peculiarity of gate-plan suggests a context for their construction and use.

The progress of a particular task-force across the landscape can be followed by observation of camps of similar size: one group of camps of 165 acres (65 ha.) has been pinpointed in Lauderdale, between the Tweed and the Forth. These camps must have held a substantial part of the army of Roman Britain and could be assigned to the campaigns of the emperor Severus in AD 209–210. Other groups of camps in Strathmore, of 63 and 130 acres (25 and 55 ha.), testify to the movements of smaller forces, perhaps also of the period of Severus (Fig. 8).

Attention can also be directed towards camps with a unique ditch system at their gateways, called 'Stracathro-type' camps from the first of the group to be recognised, beside the fort of Stracathro in Angus

14. **Dalginross, Perthshire**: aerial view of a marching camp with 'Stracathro' gateways and (to the left) a permanent fort, seen from the SW. (Photo: RCAHMS.) See also p. 157.

(Fig. 13; see also below, p.164). At one side of the gate the ditch swings out in a quarter circle (a feature known as a *clavicula*); at the other there is a short section of straight ditch angled at 45°. Such arrangements were designed to make an attack on the gateway more difficult by restricting access to it. A dozen camps with their entrances protected in this way are known, and others are suspected. From the location of some 'Stracathro' camps next to forts occupied only in the Flavian period, we can assume that they reflect the movements of Agricola's forces, or those of his immediate successor. Other camps have their gateways protected by a short length of traverse-rampart and ditch, called a *titulus* (sometimes – in my view wrongly – spelt *titulum*), placed some 10m in front of the gateway itself and lying parallel to it. Sometimes entrances were of a complexity which only excavation can disentangle. Precisely how many men could have been accommodated in any camp cannot be known, though estimates have frequently been attempted. A legion of some 5000 men seems likely to have needed a camp of about 30 acres (12 ha.) when on the march; in a

15. **Timber fort-gate**, as constructed for the serial 'The Eagle of the Ninth', near Fintry, 1977. (Photo: L. Keppie; reproduced by courtesy of BBC Scotland.)

permanent fortress it occupied about 50 acres (20 ha.). But we can never be certain of the composition of a task-force – which might comprise both infantry and cavalry, with auxiliaries as well as legionaries housed together in a single camp.

Forts

In the archaeological record, camps and forts can be easily distinguished: forts are usually small, up to 10 acres (4 ha.), and are usually defended by two or more ditches, in contrast to a single ditch round a camp; the ramparts and internal buildings of a fort are more substantial. Fort-building as such belonged to a period not of active campaigning but of the consolidation that followed. The installations which we talk of as Roman forts were built usually to house individual regiments of auxiliaries, the legions themselves residing in much larger 'fortresses' (see below, p.38). Essentially the fort provided accommodation and storage for the soldiers' gear and equipment; it was a base for their activities – we should not suppose that soldiers

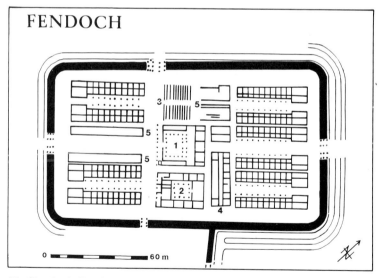

FENDOCH

0 _____ 60 m

16. **Fendoch, Perthshire**: ground-plan of the Flavian fort (after Richmond). Note: 1 = headquarters, 2 = commanding officer's house, 3 = granaries, 4 = hospital, 5 = stores. The remaining buildings are barracks. See also p. 156.

spent their service within the fort, on the defensive behind walls and gates. Rather, the fort was a jumping-off point, a base for wide-ranging activities, so that surveillance was maintained along the valleys, with patrols looking into native villages and strongpoints as required.

It has often been observed that all Roman forts look alike, but it must be stressed at once that no two are ever identical. Certainly most buildings were constructed to a standard design and their relative positions within the fort were hallowed by experience and tradition. A soldier arriving at one of the gates of a fort would know immediately, by the general layout inside, how to find the commanding officer's house, or the hospital or storebuildings, or the headquarters.

In the Flavian period the internal buildings would all have been timber-framed; archaeologically the only trace may be of post-pits or slots cut into the ground to receive horizontal sleeper-beams or to guide those erecting the principal uprights. In the Antonine period it was normal to build the headquarters building, and usually the granaries and commanding officer's house in stone, while the barracks were timber-framed.

In the centre of a fort lay the headquarters building (the *principia*), flanked on one side by the commanding officer's house (the *praetorium*) and on the other by granaries and stores, all laid out with their entrances fronting on to the main street of the fort, the *via principalis*. The remainder of the space was taken up by barracks and stables neatly aligned on the buildings of the central group.

The headquarters block is distinctive in shape: first the visitor would enter a courtyard, perhaps with rooms to either side (often these contained a weapons store). Beyond the courtyard was a covered hall, running the width of the building; at one end was a dais from which announcements could be made to those present. At the back, and opening off the covered hall, was a suite of offices, usually five rooms. The central room, whose frontage would be visible from the main door of the building, was the regimental chapel containing its standards and flags. Set into the floor there was often a strongroom or at least a timber- or stone-lined strongbox where the regiment's cash – and the soldiers' savings – were kept. Sentries in the room above protected both the standards and the cash.

The commanding officer's house stood next to the headquarters. The house was laid out to a fairly standard design – rectangular or square in shape, with rooms round four sides looking inwards to a central courtyard. Visitors to Pompeii will recognise the description, more suited to a Mediterranean climate than to northern Britain. Here the commander lived, with ample space for his wife and family, if he chose to expose them to the wild frontier.

If the commanding officer enjoyed space for relaxation and a bearable lifestyle, the soldiers – as in all ages – led the communal life of the cramped barrack room, living and eating in closely confined quarters. The barrack block housed a century of men (i.e. 80 soldiers), in ten compartments – one each for the ten squads (*contubernia*) which made up the century. There was no central cookhouse: each squad cooked as a group, with corn ground down on hand-querns and taken for baking to an oven set at the back of the rampart.

On the Scottish frontier barracks were normally timber-framed with walls of wattles (rather like modern garden fencing) coated with clay. The roofs were of timber slatting, or thatch. The barrack-rooms all had their doors opening on to the same side of the block, where there was often a verandah. At one end of the block, usually that nearer the rampart, was a small suite of three or four rooms where the centurion in command had his quarters.

The buildings which housed the fort's food supply – usually called 'granaries' – are easily recognised on the ground by their elongated shape, and in the Antonine period by their side-buttresses and solid stone construction. The floors – of laid paving slabs – were raised off the ground on low 'dwarf' walls, allowing the air to pass beneath, through ventilation slots in the side walls. Set into the walls were large louvred windows, and the structure had a heavy overhanging roof. Granaries were thus well designed and expertly built to keep their contents dry and clear of frost and rodents.

Another important building for the garrison was the bath-house, which might lie inside the fort up against the rampart, or outside it in an annexe; the bath-house was normally kept away from other buildings to lessen the fire risk from its furnaces. The bath-house, which was always stone-built, consisted of a sequence of rooms heated to varying temperatures. The bather entered first a cold room, then proceeded through rooms of increasingly higher temperatures, thereafter retracing his steps to the cold room, where water splashed over the body served to close up the pores before the bather dressed and came out again into the open air. Often there was a hot dry 'sauna' room as well. The floors were raised off the ground on a sequence of small pillars or brick stacks (the *hypocaust* system of underfloor heating), and heat supplied from one or more furnaces. Heat was also

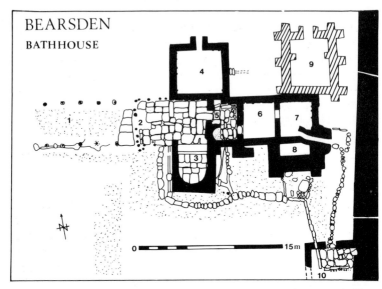

17. **Bearsden on the Antonine wall**: the fort-bathhouse (after Breeze). Note 1 = changing room, 2 = cold room, 3 = cold plunge bath, 4 = hot dry room, 5–6 = warm rooms, 7 = hot room, 8 = hot bath, 9 = heated room(?), 10 = latrine. See also p. 135.

18. **Leisure and recreation**. Gaming board from Bearsden; counters from Newstead; strigil (for scraping off dirt) from Bar Hill; unguent pots from Balmuildy. (Photo: Hunterian Museum.)

carried up the walls in sets of square-sectioned pipes (called box-flues). A bath-house is always instantly recognisable on excavation, from the appearance of the hypocausts, or large areas of burning near the furnaces or from fragments of the orange-red box-flues, which often survive in vast quantities. The bath-house was usually quite a small building, and we must suppose a strict rota for access. Soldiers played dice, chatted about their families and homes, and whiled away the off-duty hours.

Larger forts might have a hospital, with wards arranged to either side of a central corridor, and workshops for the repair of vehicles, weapons and tools.

Roman forts on the Scottish frontier often had attached to them annexes, that is enclosures defended by a rampart and ditch, on one or more sides of the fort. Such annexes have not been excavated extensively, but where examined they have been found to contain hearths and ovens, and workshops for industrial activities, as well as religious shrines and sometimes, as already indicated, the fort bath-house. We should not suppose that they were mere empty space.

The defences of a fort consisted of a rampart, usually of turf with (in the Antonine period) a stone foundation-course. Beyond (i.e. outside) the rampart were one or more ditches, usually about 3m across and 1.5m deep. Gaps were left in the ditch-circuit for roads leading into the fort. The fort-gates were substantial timber structures, usually with a tower above the gate-passage itself, or towers at either side.

Outside the fort some civilian structures could be expected, to house the families and slaves of the soldiers, friendly natives (some of whom could well have chosen to live for their own safety in the lee of the fort), and traders and storekeepers providing extra food, luxuries and various services to the soldiers of the garrison. Wine and women were presumably available at a price, and songs inspired by the former and describing the latter were doubtless to be heard. These little villages grew up along the roads leading away from the forts. We do not as yet know very much about civilian settlements in Scotland, although they are familiar to the visitor to Hadrian's Wall, for example at Housesteads and Vindolanda.

Fortlets

A very much smaller installation was the fortlet: a mini-version of the

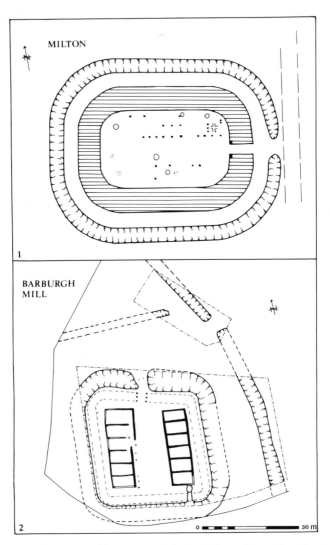

19. **Fortlets of the Antonine period**. 1. Milton, Dumfriesshire (after Clarke), showing postholes of internal buildings, within a rampart and single ditch; see also p. 82. 2. Barburgh Mill, Dumfriesshire (after Breeze), showing plans of two barracks within a rampart (outline restored) and a single ditch. The extra ditches to the N and E restricted access to the promontory on which the fortlet sat; see also p. 86.

full-sized fort, designed to house 50 to 80 men at most in one or two barrack blocks. Fortlets usually had a single gate through the rampart, with a timber tower above, and one or two ditches beyond. Fortlets are found in Scotland at intermediate points along major roads, or at river crossings. One particular type of fortlet appears on the Antonine Wall – seemingly at every mile there was a fortlet-type structure attached to the Wall itself; we call these small installations 'mile-fortlets' (below, p.117). They match the milecastles on Hadrian's Wall and served as intermediate control points along the frontier line.

Watch-towers

Mention should also be made of watch-towers: these were usually of

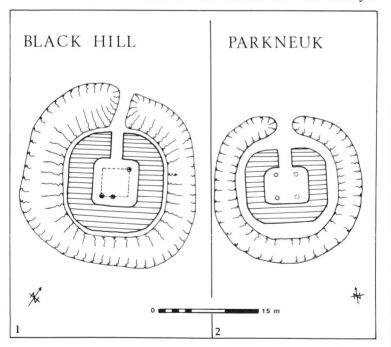

20. **Watch-towers of the Flavian period**. 1. Black Hill, Meikleour, Perthshire (after Richmond): a tower 12 ft (3.5m) square lay within a broad turf rampart and a single ditch; see also p. 163. 2. Parkneuk, Gask Ridge, Perthshire (after Robertson). The tower 10 ft (3m) square lay within a rampart and single ditch; see also p. 150.

timber, set within a low rampart and a single or double ditch, and spaced out along roads to observe traffic and population movement. Most towers were some 3m square at the base, and at least two storeys high. A causeway led through the ditch or ditches to the nearby road. These towers may have been manned by half a dozen men, perhaps a dozen at most. We could easily worry about their safety in the event of a sudden attack by substantial hostile forces. Information would be passed by means of fire-signals or torches along a line of such posts to warn of danger. On the Gask Ridge in Perthshire a regular sequence of towers seems to have served for a time to mark the outer limit of the Roman province in the Flavian period (below, p. 42).

Legionary fortresses

For the most part, after an initial conquest period, the legions returned to their bases in the south, while the auxiliaries in their forts remained scattered through the countryside and along lines of communication. Nevertheless Scotland can boast of two legionary fortresses – at Inchtuthil on the Tay near Dunkeld (below, p.160), and at Carpow on the southern side of the Tay estuary near Newburgh (below, p.153). Inchtuthil belongs to the period of the Flavian occupation in the later 1st century and Carpow to the Severan advance in the early 3rd. So far as we can tell, no legion was based in Scotland in the Antonine period, though some legionaries remained as garrisons in a few of the Antonine Wall forts, at Newstead and perhaps elsewhere.

A legionary fortress was a fort on a very large scale indeed; or rather the *fort* was a microcosm of the legionary base. The legionary fortresses of the Roman world were about 50–60 acres in size, and housed some 5000 men. The reader will recognise the main features of the layout of Inchtuthil (Fig.21): headquarters building, granaries, store buildings, a hospital, and barracks in profusion, arranged in groups of six, reflecting the six centuries of the legionary cohort. Lacking at Inchtuthil is the commanding officer's house, evidently not yet built when the base was abandoned.

Roads

Of vital importance to the Roman control of a frontier area was a

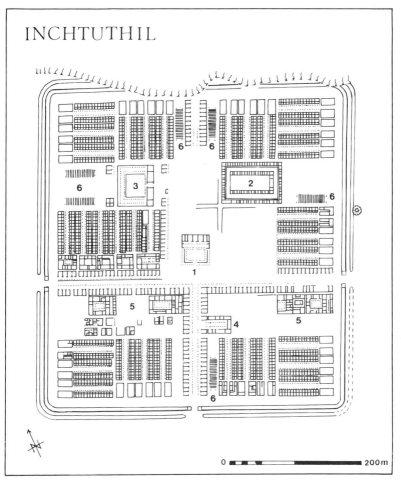

INCHTUTHIL

21. **Inchtuthil, Perthshire**: ground-plan of a legionary fortress of the Flavian period (after Pitts and St. Joseph). Note: 1 = headquarters, 2 = hospital, 3 = workshop, 4 = drill-hall(?), 5 = tribunes' houses, 6 = granaries. The remaining buildings are barracks. See also Fig. 86.

network of roads. 'All roads lead to Rome' is a familiar saying. More correctly all roads led *from* Rome, reaching out from the city to Italian towns and then to provincial centres and from there to the very frontiers of the Empire. In Britain the road system developed quickly in the aftermath of the Claudian conquest. Roads radiated from

22. **Roman road** at Stonehouse, Lanarkshire, looking E along its embankment; the alignment is continued by the line of trees into the distance. (Photo: L. Keppie.) See also p. 99.

London, to the West Country, into the Midlands (Watling Street) and due northwards to York (Ermine Street). In Scotland the network of roads was determined by topographical necessities (below, p.42), along the valleys still used for the most part by the modern road and rail networks. Roman roads are found today by recognition of their cambered mounds in the countryside; by observation on maps of the alignment of secondary roads, farm-tracks, or field boundaries; by the identification of placenames indicating old roads; and from the air – a whiteish parched stripe indicating the presence of a gravel surface not far below the present-day ground-level, or quarry pits and drainage gullies extending into the distance across the landscape.

Excavation reveals a fairly standard make-up: a lower stratum of large cobbles, some 6m across, topped by small stones and gravel, and often flanked by drainage gullies. Sometimes the road was set on a bed of turf, or placed directly on rock. The essentials of the road system must have been laid down by Agricola or his immediate successor: some lengths of road north of Perth must be dated to this time, as the area was not seemingly reoccupied in the Antonine period. Roman roads are proverbial for their straightness. More often the road-

23. **Milestone**, from Ingliston, West Lothian. (Photo: National Museums of Scotland.) See also p. 111.

builders (usually soldiers) marked out a line in advance from one high point to another, after which there might be a change in alignment. By geographical necessity Roman roads in Scotland were often not straight, especially when following a river. Distances along the roads were marked by milestones, of which only one has survived from Scotland – at Ingliston near Edinburgh (below, p.111). As Scotland had at least 500 miles of Roman road, many more milestones must await discovery.

CHAPTER 5

The Monuments in the Landscape

For the Roman army, as much as for later English invaders and the modern traveller and tourist, the approaches to Scotland by land are strictly limited by, and must conform to, geographical factors. The modern traveller to Scotland, whether by road or rail, follows the valleys of the Annan and the Clyde to reach Glasgow. On the eastern side of the country the traveller from Newcastle to the Forth at Edinburgh may follow the coast (the A1), or strike inland by way of Redesdale across Carter Bar to the Tweed Valley and then via Lauderdale to the Forth (the modern A68).

Further north the major arterial route runs from Falkirk to Stirling, then through Strathallan to the Tay at Perth. Thereafter the traveller must traverse the low lands of Strathmore, noting always the heights of the Highland massif on his left, mountains which draw ever closer until the mouths of the Dee and the Don, after which the plains of Moray and Nairn come into view.

To the modern reader and traveller, with satellite pictures of Scotland available in every atlas, and Ordnance Survey maps providing an easy digest of available knowledge, such a statement on routes may seem obvious enough. The best way from Glasgow to Edinburgh, or Carlisle to the Clyde, may be obvious from an aircraft or even from an armchair, but the Romans had no such advantages. Dependent on reconnaisance parties, hearsay and features visible on the horizon, they proceeded to lay down the essentials of a communication system that has lasted until the present day.

It seems clear that the Romans did not think merely in terms of north–south communication. A significant geographical, and indeed geological, factor in the make-up of the Scottish terrain is the sequences of hills that run north–east to south–west: the Cheviots, the Lammermuirs, the Pentlands south of the Forth, and further north the Ochils and the Highland massif. That the Romans in the Flavian period established a north–east to south–west defence line along the edge of the Highlands has always been evident. But south of the Forth

42

their road network, both confirmed by actual survivals and restored by reasonable conjecture, suggests a number of lines running north–east to south–west which may mark stages in advance or withdrawal, or at the very least of communication and control between tribal groupings, in the 1st and 2nd centuries.

Many Roman installations are immediately recognisable on the ground or from the air. Forts, with their multiple ditches, 'playing card' shape, rounded corners and regular street plans; camps with long straight ditches, symmetrically placed gateways defended by *clavicula* or by traverse (above, p.29); the roads with their confident alignment, quarry pits and side-ditches. But not every square enclosure need be a Roman fort or fortlet, and not every circular ditch seen from the air need enclose a Roman watch-tower. Rigorous modern research into the characteristics of field monuments has removed doubt in many cases, but it would be premature to claim that every archaeological site seen in the countryside or observed from the air can be instantly categorised. Proximity to a Roman road could decide in favour of a Roman date – yet a ditched enclosure at West Plean beside a Roman road north of Larbert, excavated in 1953–55 to provide a plan of a Roman watch-tower, proved instead to be an Iron Age homestead. A ditched enclosure on Beattock summit, initially considered by some as a burial cairn, was found on excavation in 1966 to be a Roman watch-tower (below, p. 83). From the air such small enclosures, with a circular ditch interrupted by a single gap, may be hard to categorise. Square enclosures with sharp rather than round corners may prove to enclose Iron Age or mediaeval settlements or homesteads. Sometimes aerial reconnaisance can reveal sites of many different periods in close proximity: the same factors (well-drained ground, water supply, a river crossing) could bring not only Romans but prehistoric settlers, and motte- and castle-builders later. The Romans were not alone in building roads in Scotland: mediaeval hollow-ways and 18th-century metalled roads may run parallel to, or overlie or disrupt, the Roman system. Not every straight road need be Roman. Indeed one stretch of paved road with a central drain, descending a steep slope near Rochdale in Lancashire, which has often been illustrated in books about Roman Britain, is now known to have been laid down in 1734!

CHAPTER 6

Piecing Together the Roman Past

The source material available for a study of the Romans in Scotland does not consist merely of literary works surviving from antiquity. We have already learned something of the structural evidence deriving from the excavated remains of forts and other installations. The process of excavation produces in addition a sometimes considerable quantity of artefacts in metal, stone, clay, glass and other materials, all of which can provide information to the historian or archaeologist. Some of these categories of finds deserve a detailed description.

a. Inscriptions

Particularly helpful towards our appreciation of the Roman period in Scotland are inscriptions, that is stones on which have been inscribed some words or phrases in Latin. The language is not the literary Latin of Tacitus, Cicero or Vergil; rather the texts abound with semi-technical phrases of the military establishment. Words are often abbreviated, even to a single letter. Such abbreviations must, we may safely assume, have been comprehensible to Roman soldiers but may require some hard thinking for us to decipher today. Yet we too live in a world of abbreviations – some are perennial, for example a.m. and p.m. (derived from Latin); others are potentially short-lived, for example VAT or MOT, which in a generation or two will perhaps be all but forgotten, to remain only of mild antiquarian interest. Abbreviations were used on Latin inscriptions primarily to save space, so enabling the writer to maximise the content of the message on the limited flat area of stone available.

The most common categories of inscriptions are a. commemorative stones recording building work; b. altars erected to gods and goddesses; and c. gravestones, chiefly of members of the Roman garrisons or their families. Almost all the inscriptions known in Roman Scotland belong in the Antonine period, i.e. in the mid-2nd century AD.

24. Inscribed stones from the Antonine Wall (after Collingwood and Wright). 1. Distance slab from Kirkintilloch erected by men of the Sixth Legion (Scale 1/24); the actual length of the Wall completed by the legion was never inserted on the stone. 2. Altar from Auchendavy near Kirkintilloch, erected to the Presiding Spirit (*genius*) of the Land of Britain by Marcus Cocceius Firmus, a centurion of the Second Legion (see also p. 132). Scale 1/16. 3. Gravestone from Shirva near Kirkintilloch, commemorating Flavius Lucianus, a soldier in the Second Legion. Scale 1/16. The original stones are in the Hunterian Museum.

Commemorative stones, the first category, are usually rectangular in shape and relatively thin, and were intended to be inserted into the building whose construction they recorded. The inscription was placed on the front face of the stone, often within a moulded frame. The inscription normally began with the name and titles of the reigning emperor: IMP(ERATORI) CAES(ARI) T(ITO) AE(LIO) HADR(IANO) ANTONINO AVG(VSTO) PIO P(ATRI) P(ATRIAE). That is 'For the Emperor Caesar Titus Aelius Hadrianus Antoninus Augustus Pius, Father of the Nation'. The word *imperator* is our 'Emperor', which appeared on British coinage up to 1949, when King George VI ceased to employ the designation IND(IAE) IMP(ERATOR), Emperor of India. The title 'Caesar' had originally been the surname of a particular individual, Julius Caesar, but under the Roman Empire it became a title, to be borne by each emperor in turn. So too the name Augustus, 'the hallowed one', a title which had been awarded to the first Roman emperor. This title was adopted by later rulers and helped to legitimise their rule. 'Titus' was the forename of Antoninus himself. Both 'Aelius' and 'Hadrianus' were the names of Antoninus' predecessor, Hadrian. Antoninus added them to his own, when Hadrian adopted him a few months before his own death. 'Antoninus Pius' is the name we know and use today. A reputation for 'loyalty' brought him the designation *Pius* ('loyal', the original meaning of the Latin word). Finally comes the abbreviation P P for *pater patriae*, 'Father of the Nation', a title often adopted today by the Presidents of emergent countries. For the Romans, it reflected the emperor's position as 'head of state'.

A building inscription next provides details of the legion or auxiliary regiment responsible for the work, for example VEX(ILLATIO) LEG(IONIS) II AVG(VSTAE) – a detachment of the Second Augustan Legion; or COH(ORS) I TVNGR(ORVM) – the First Cohort of Tungrians. Usually the inscription ends at this point, without actually saying *what* was built – there was no particular need to take up space with that piece of information, as the slab would have been set into a wall or above a door of the building whose construction was being commemorated.

One particular category of commemorative stones deserves a special mention: the so-called 'distance slabs' from the Antonine Wall, which record the lengths of wall-building work completed by the legionary detachments engaged on the task. Here the inscriptions begin with a dedication to the emperor Antoninus Pius, then give the numeral and the titles of the legion responsible, and end with the precise distance completed, in paces or in feet (see Fig 24.1, Figs 74–75).

A second category of stones is *altars*, squat squared-off pillars which bear an inscription to the god or goddess being venerated. The top of an altar was hollowed out to form a *focus* or miniature hearth where fruit might be piled as an offering. The dedicator then poured wine or milk on top. On large altars a fire might be lit in the *focus* to consume the offerings, but it is evident that the *focus* on many altars is just too

25. **Sacrifice at an altar**. A scene from the distance slab found at Bridgeness. (See also Fig. 6.) Here officers and soldiers of the Second Legion (note flag in background with name of legion) offer sacrifice, probably to Mars, to ask for the god's support in the forthcoming campaign. (Photo: National Museums of Scotland.)

small to have served that purpose – the hollow was merely symbolic. Sometimes, if the occasion was sufficiently important or the dedicator sufficiently wealthy, an animal might be sacrificed, and its flesh burnt on the altar.

Altars were not erected on the spur of the moment. What happened was that someone (an individual or a group) might promise an altar to a god, if the god gave some help in a time of need – for example to

Neptune before a sea-crossing or to Mars before a battle. If the desired help was forthcoming and the person came safely through the expected ordeal, he erected an altar in fulfilment of the promise. The inscription on an altar first named the god to whom the dedication was being made, then the names of the dedicators (if a whole military unit set up the altar, the commanding officer's name was given), and ended with the standard formula *votum solvit laetus libens merito* (always abbreviated to the lettrs VSLLM): 'gladly, willingly and deservedly fulfilled his vow'; i.e. the vow to erect the altar which had been made when the god's help was first asked for.

The deities commemorated in this way might be the gods and goddesses of the Roman world – such as Jupiter, king of the gods, Juno his wife (especially venerated by women), Mars, god of war, or Minerva, goddess of valour. Sometimes more exotic gods of the eastern Mediterranean and beyond are found on the northern frontier in Britain. These eastern deities offered a more exciting concept of religion, and rituals in which the individual had a definite role. At other times the dedications are to the local Celtic deities of the woodland and the stream. Auxiliary regiments dedicated altars to the deities of their homelands far away; for example, at Birrens in Dumfriesshire, the Second Cohort of Tungrians from Belgium set up altars to the outlandish-sounding goddesses Viradecthis and Ricagambeda. Sometimes Roman and Celtic deities were worshipped together; at Bar Hill on the Antonine Wall a cohort of Syrian archers from the town of Hama on the Orontes river put up a dedication to Mars Camulus, the Roman and Celtic war-gods combined as a single personage. From Croy Hill on the Antonine Wall there is a dedication to Jupiter Dolichenus, that is to the Syrian god of the heavens equated with Jupiter; such was the all-embracing and cosmopolitan nature of religious belief in antiquity (see Fig. 38).

Gravestones form a third category of inscription. The text is usually quite short: the name of the deceased and his military unit, perhaps the number of years served and the age at death. Sometimes the inscription may be accompanied by a full-length sculptured representation of the deceased, in uniform. The gravestones were erected along the roads leading away from forts, often in a special plot.

The gravestones marked the last resting place of the body – or more usually the ashes – of the deceased, cremation being the normal rite at this time. Gravestones cost money, and not everyone could afford them: ashes might simply be placed in a glass jar or in an earthenware

26. **Cremation burial in a pot**; found at Croy Hill, 1976. (Photo: Hunterian Museum.)

pot, with a wooden marker, or none at all, at ground level. Soldiers contributed during service to a burial-club which ensured proper commemoration if the need arose.

It should be emphasised that not every inscription survives complete – sometimes only a fragment is found with a few letters legible, where the message breaks off tantalisingly in mid-word or phrase. Several stones reported by antiquarians can no longer be found, or the inscription cannot now be read, after prolonged exposure to rain and frost. Many stones found long ago were built into farmhouses, and perished when the latter were rebuilt in Victorian times or later.

Not every Latin inscription was chiselled on stone: words could be scratched on pots, stamped on tiles, or engraved on glass and metal. Samian pottery (below, p.54) often bears the name of the maker or his factory, as do *mortaria* (mixing bowls); amphorae often have a stamp on the rim or handle indicating the name of the estate where the contents – oil or wine – were produced. Sometimes the owners of pots wrote their own names on the side, or scratched a mark to indicate the current contents – for example VIN for *vinum* (wine). From Carpow comes an amphora with a graffito which seems to indicate that the contents were flavoured with horehound, evidently as cough mixture, no doubt much in demand on the cold northern frontier. Such casual scribblings often cast a highly informative light.

b. Coins

Many families in Britain today have a Roman coin somewhere at home, perhaps several, to show to children and visitors as relics of a past era; sometimes these are coins found in Scotland itself, but others have been brought back from abroad, often by returning servicemen, or bought in antique shops. Coins were first brought to Scotland in bulk by the Roman soldiers of the invasion army, and by the commissariat officers who used them to pay for materials and foodstuffs purchased locally. Roman coins bore on the obverse (heads) side the profile of the reigning emperor, and on the reverse (tails) side perhaps the outline of a newly completed public building, for example the Colosseum, which was opened to the public in AD 80 while Agricola was in Scotland. A Caledonian bear, perhaps furnished through the agency of Agricola's army, was among the attractions at the inaugural games; or the news of some military victory or information about the imperial family. Coins served like our postage stamps today as a digest of recent events. They were a convenient method of propagating information to the population of a far-flung empire. Round the edge of the coin was an inscription giving on the obverse the names and titles of the emperor, and the magistracies he had held or was then holding, and on the reverse some brief message, just a word or two, explaining the scene portrayed.

Sometimes the events reported on the reverses of coins referred to Britain or victories won there. Thus the successes of Lollius Urbicus'

27. **Bronze arm-purse, with coins**. The purse was found at Croy Hill in 1978. (Photo: Hunterian Museum.)

army in Scotland in AD 142–43 prompted the issue of coins showing Britannia reclining on rocks, and others with a winged victory-figure and the letters BRITAN. Similarly the achievements of the emperor Severus and his son Caracalla in Britain in AD 208–211 were reported on their coins, with scenes showing victory-figures piling up captured arms, and the legend VICTORIAE BRITANNICAE; 'victories won over the Britons'. By the time that many of these coins were brought into circulation, it is very likely that the Roman army had already left Scotland and given up its conquests!

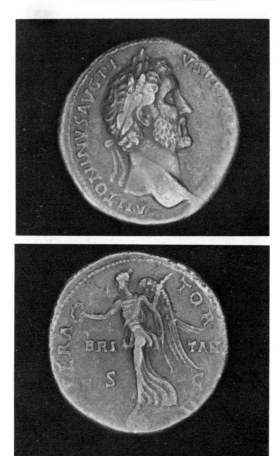

28. Coin (*sestertius*) of Antoninus Pius, commemorating the reconquest of Scotland, issued AD 143–44. (a) obverse showing head of Antoninus; (b) reverse showing personification of Victory with a laurel wreath, and the legend BRITAN, i.e. Britannia. (Photos: Hunter Coin Cabinet.)

Coins are found on excavations of Roman sites in Scotland, but not in large numbers. Others are casual finds, from gardens or ploughed fields. Nowadays many coins found each year are located by metal detectors. Finders are required by law to report such material to the police or to a museum, but it appears that in many cases the finder does not pass the information on, so that no proper record is made and the full significance of the find is lost. Most of the coins found in the

29. Coin (*sestertius*) of Caracalla, commemorating the Severan campaigns in Scotland, issued AD 211. (a) obverse showing head of Caracalla; (b) reverse showing Victory piling up captured weaponry, with the legend VICT BRIT, i.e. Victoriae Britannicae (victories won in Britain). (Photos: Hunter Coin Cabinet.)

ground are very corroded and need expert attention if they are to be identified and dated and not to disintegrate from handling and from contact with the air.

c. Miscellaneous small finds

Inscriptions and coins were not the only artefacts left behind by the Romans in Scotland. A visitor walking over a Roman site is most likely to pick up fragments of pottery brought to the surface by

30. **Table ware**. Bronze jug from Lesmahagow, and samian vessels. (Photo: Hunterian Museum.)

ploughing. On an excavation the pottery will form the bulk of the finds made during the dig. What we see is the crockery of the barrack room and the cooking area. Of all Roman pottery the most distinctive is so-called samian ware, which was imported to Britain from central and southern France. The name 'samian' results from a mistaken inference made years ago about its place of manufacture, then believed to be the Greek island of Samos. Samian ware was made in many standard shapes: cups, plates and bowls (the latter often decorated with embossed designs). It is frequently possible to assign even the smallest fragment to a particular type of vessel, so standardised were the shapes.

Another common find is the *mortarium*, a heavy-rimmed bowl used for mixing and crushing vegetables. It resembles the modern baking-bowl, but was clearly not used for baking: the interior had a coating of rough quartz-grit which helped to break down vegetables, but wore away in time and must have ended up in the food itself.

Equally distinctive is the bulbous amphora, with its strong handles and broad rim, the bulk container of antiquity (it held about 6 gallons/

31. **Cooking vessels**. *Mortarium* (mixing bowl), jars and dishes. (Photo: Hunterian Museum.)

27 litres). The amphorae found in Britain came mostly from southern Spain, and were used to export that country's most plentiful products, olive oil (for cooking) and wine.

In addition the Roman soldiers had available a wide range of jars and cooking pots, among them 'black-burnished ware' made in Dorset and in Essex, 'Severn Valley' ware from the Avon area, and locally produced vessels. Pottery kilns have been found in recent years at several forts in Scotland, indicating that the supplies from the south might be supplemented by wares produced locally as the demand arose.

An excavation is likely also to yield some ironwork – brackets, hinges and the like, but most frequently nails. There may also be a few objects of bronze – belt-fittings, horse-trappings and brooches. Lead was used, as in modern times, for piping. Frequently too there is glass – mainly from window panes, in a shiny blue-green colour, clear on one side and frosted on the other; less frequently fragments of glass bottles and cups are found – needless to say these must have been easily broken. Finally the archaeologist on an excavation or the walker over a ploughed field may find fragments of roofing tiles in a hard red clay, and bricks and flue-tiles, the wreckage of a hypocaust (above, p.35).

Other luxury items too may be found – finger rings with engraved gemstones set into them, or jewellery in glass, silver or gold. A few wooden objects may also be recovered during excavation, preserved in wet conditions, the remnants of a wide range of structural timbers, fitments, furniture and personal belongings which have crumbled away over the centuries. Complete wagon-wheels have been found at Bar Hill and at Newstead. Leather too can survive if the surroundings are sufficiently damp: both Newstead and Bar Hill have produced shoes by the score, and we may also see today in museums leather panels from soldiers' tents, and fragments of clothing and shield covers, even a satchel.

When isolated finds are made, the finder often (though unfortunately not always) brings the material to a museum or to an archaeologist who will be able to identify it. All genuine finds – and of course not every object believed by its finder to be Roman is that old or was actually found in Scotland – are reported in *Discovery & Excavation in Scotland*, a yearly magazine (published by the Council for British Archaeology Scotland), through which the information is disseminated to a wider public. Finds may be made by walkers in the countryside, or by farmers in newly ploughed fields; or by metal detector users. Sometimes the finds are from known Roman sites – where a tree has blown over or a stream is eroding a bank or hillside; or are found completely in isolation where no known site exists. Individual discoveries may seem isolated, but the archaeologist will know whether there is a Roman site nearby. Sometimes apparently isolated finds are shown years later to derive from a Roman fort which was not yet located when the find was made: the find itself may be the first indicator of the existence of a site. Every find should not be taken to indicate a Roman installation: sometimes coins or potsherds, rings or brooches were lost beside a road, the result of traffic along it. Or the material may prove to derive from a village or homestead of the native population, who had obtained Roman goods, as gifts or bribes, by exchange or barter, as they became aware of the proximity of the manufactured goods of the Roman common market. Roman material reached native sites not only within the areas under the army's control; Roman objects are found in the far North, in the Outer Isles and in Orkney and Shetland, the result of trade and contact over many hundreds of miles.

CHAPTER 7

The Rediscovery of Roman Scotland

Today we are familiar with the names of many archaeological sites and their precise dating within the Roman period. But for the antiquarians of many centuries ago, the picture was much less clear.

Already by the fall of the Roman Empire in the 5th century AD, Roman historians were becoming confused about who had actually built walls in Britain and where they were. But gradually, with the rediscovery of classical manuscripts in the monasteries of continental Europe, it could be seen that Scotland had indeed been invaded and occupied on a number of occasions. Early Scottish historians endeavoured to reconcile popular tradition with the newly available literary evidence. Yet even the location of the Antonine Wall remained a matter of dispute until 1684, when an inscribed stone bearing the name of Lollius Urbicus was found at Balmuildy fort. This stone, claimed antiquarian Alexander Gordon, was 'the most invaluable Jewel of Antiquity that ever was found in the Island of Britain'. Today's students would be amazed to think that the siting of the Wall, between Clyde and Forth, had ever been in doubt.

By the early 17th century inscriptions were being read and their texts published; the standing remains were being pinpointed on the ground. The 18th century was a period of great antiquarian activity. In 1726 Alexander Gordon published his *Itinerarium Septentrionale* (Journey through the North) which recorded in set sequence many Roman sites in Scotland, with sketch-plans of the sites and drawings of associated antiquities. This volume was followed shortly by the ambitious and authoritative *Britannia Romana* of John Horsley whose survey covered all of Roman Britain, with emphasis on Hadrian's Wall and the North. The role of Scotland in the history of the Roman Empire was now firmly established.

Among Scottish antiquarians of this time the dominant figure was Sir John Clerk of Penicuik whose indefatigable efforts are recorded in a voluminous correspondence with fellow enthusiasts; the outbuildings at Penicuik House soon overflowed with altars and inscribed

32. 'The most invaluable Jewel of Antiquity' (Alexander Gordon). Commemorative tablet from Balmuildy fort on the Antonine Wall, recording construction work by the Second Legion during the governorship of Quintus Lollius Urbicus. (Photo: Hunterian Museum.)

stones sent to him by admirers and friends. Many of the inscribed stones assembled by Clerk passed in 1857 to the then National Museum of Antiquities in Edinburgh.

The aftermath of the second Jacobite Rebellion of 1745 brought to Scotland a young surveyor of the first order, William Roy, who assisted in the laying out of new roads to control the Highlands; he also worked on the preparation of a large-scale map of Scotland. Roy noted the surviving earthworks of many sites he recognised as of Roman origin, and had them accurately planned; the end product was *The Military Antiquities of the Romans in Britain*, published (after his death) in 1793. Many of the sites drawn under Roy's direction are now badly eroded or even afforested, so that his survey may supply details long since lost. The zest for antiquarian discovery in the 18th century is reflected in Sir Walter Scott's novel, *The Antiquary*, published in 1816. At one point the hero, Jonathan Oldbuck, proudly displays to a visitor the battlefield of *Mons Graupius* which lay, he claimed, on his own estate.

The antiquarians of the 18th and 19th centuries put together their picture of Roman Scotland by the observation and recording of

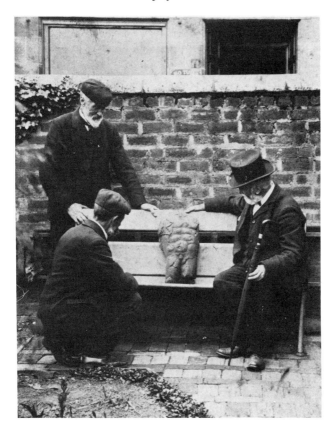

33. Antiquarians examining a newly found Roman torso from Camelon, 1905. (Photo: Falkirk Museum.)

standing monuments, together with an account of the Roman finds, especially inscribed stones and coins, made at each site over the years. But, perhaps surprisingly to the modern reader, they did not dig in search of information. The pen, the measuring chain and the surveyor's pole were their tools, not the spade, the trowel or the brush. Perhaps we should be grateful for this – most sites were left alone until more modern methods became available. The 1890s brought a decisive change: the Society of Antiquaries of Scotland established a committee to plan and carry out excavations on selected important sites, and within a ten-year period large-scale work took place at many forts. The results received prompt publication in the *Proceedings of the*

34. Glenlochar, Kirkcudbright. Outline of the Roman fort showing as a crop-mark, seen from the W (Photo: Ministry of Defence, British Crown Copyright Reserved).

Society of Antiquaries of Scotland. Much was learned in a short span of time. At about the same time a committee of the Glasgow Archaeological Society carried out a more modest programme of work along the line of the Antonine Wall, to confirm its alignment and examine its constituent parts. The resulting *Antonine Wall Report* (1899) is still valuable today for its careful observations and thoughtful conclusions.

In the present century excavation has continued apace. Special mention can be made of the work of Sir George Macdonald at several Antonine Wall sites, which culminated in his *Roman Wall in Scotland* (second edition, Oxford 1934). Sir Ian Richmond dug with masterly brilliance at Inchtuthil and Fendoch, and at many other sites north and south of the Antonine Wall. More recently has come the work of

Professor Anne Robertson at Castledykes, Duntocher, Birrens and elsewhere. Their colleagues and successors have maintained the momentum.

Emphasis has shifted from excavation purely for the purposes of gaining information, to 'rescue' archaeology, on sites threatened by destruction from modern development, whether for oil pipelines, roads, factories or housing projects. Such rescue excavation attracts government funding – obviously an allurement now that excavation has become an extremely expensive activity, with the employment of mechanical excavators to speed the process when time (or rather the lack of it) is an important factor. The costs of post-excavation work are high too, now that the botanist, the soil scientist, the conservation technician and a variety of specialist workers can be recruited to study the small finds and ecological setting of the site. As the techniques of excavation have improved, the process of digging has paradoxically slowed. New sites are being found faster than they can possibly be excavated, so that there is no danger of today's archaeologists running out of projects.

The number of known sites has expanded enormously since 1900, and new discoveries seem likely to continue at an undiminished rate. Gaps are being filled on the map of Roman Scotland, new roads are being identified, and the whole picture of occupation appears more intense. New sites are still found by observation on the ground, as in past decades, by the dedicated fieldworker, following a fine tradition exemplified by O. G. S. Crawford, one-time Archaeology Officer of the Ordnance Survey. Many more sites have, however, been identified from the air.

The realisation that ancient sites might be visible from the air when nothing can be seen at ground level developed in the inter-war years as the potential of the aircraft was perceived. The Second World War saw an improvement in techniques, and post-war examination of many photographs taken for military purposes revealed a plethora of archaeological sites. An annual programme of flying was initiated by Dr. (now Professor) J. K. S. St. Joseph to cover much of Britain. In Scotland Professor St. Joseph has added by his own efforts well over 20 forts and fortlets and dozens of marching camps to the map. Observation from the air was followed by the testing of the sites on the ground by carefully placed trenches. Latterly St. Joseph's work has been continued by Gordon Maxwell and his colleagues at the Royal Commission on the Ancient and Historical Monuments of Scotland, with the aid of government grants.

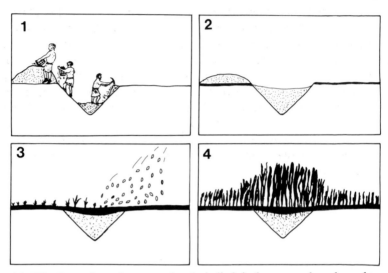

35. **The formation of crop-marks**. 1. A ditch is dug out and earth used to create a rampart. 2. The ditch fills up (or is filled in) over the centuries. 3. A farmer plants a crop. 4. Seeds planted over the line of the ditch grow better because of the extra moisture below. (After an original drawing by Maggie Wallace.)

Ancient sites can show up from the air because raking sunlight accentuates the faint remains of ramparts and ditches, which may be all that survive at ground level. Alternatively a light coating of snow may highlight the ancient features, or the differential melting of that snow may reveal a pattern. Much more common are what are called 'cropmark' sites, where certain features, especially ditches, show up from the air because of differential growth in a crop. The reason for this difference is that ditches dug long ago into the ground to defend a camp or fort attract water and moisture, so that at the height of summer when the crop – barley or wheat, even vegetables – is ripening, those parts of the crop overlying the now vanished ditches will grow thicker and higher, and remain unripened for a few days, perhaps a few weeks, longer than the rest of the field. From the air the line of the ditch shows up as a green strip in the field where everything else has turned a golden yellow or begun to wither. It would be difficult to overstate the contribution of aerial photography to our knowledge of Roman Scotland. Yet it is perhaps not always easy for the general public to perceive its importance, when the end product of the investigation is not pottery, stone structures or the like, but a photographic print, in which certain lines and blobs are proclaimed significant by the finder and others dismissed as drainage ditches, hayricks and geological features. But photographs may speak eloquently of the impact of the Roman presence in Scotland, especially when a whole fort may be brought within our view, with its rounded corners, its gates, the orderly lines of streets and buildings, all this when nothing may be seen at ground level and no excavation has ever been undertaken at the site (Fig. 34). Given the ever-spiralling costs of excavation, aerial reconnaisance has proved an economical method of identifying new sites.

CHAPTER 8

Life on the Frontier

What can we say about life on Rome's most northerly frontier? Throughout the periods of Roman rule, Scotland was under a strong military occupation, so that much of what we know relates to army personnel in their official duties and off-duty moments.

Life in forts in Roman Scotland, and on the Antonine Wall, was surely like that endured by defenders of frontiers anywhere – isolated and uneventful, or like army service today likely to consist of long periods of inaction punctuated by short spasms of intense activity, exhilaration and danger. This excess of inactivity was guarded against by Roman commanders who devised a number of expedients to counter it: route marches, arms training, practising the building of ramparts and the digging of ditches, even mock battles. It was this attitude of professionalism that made the Roman army superior to its opponents for so long. A degree of alertness had to be simulated when the army was converted to a frontier police force with every risk of staleness.

We can build up from the archaeological assemblage a picture of life in the forts themselves: the crockery used, the food eaten and the living conditions. Analysis of sewage deposits at Bearsden has provided information on the soldiers' diet (below p.138). In general the soldiers lived on dairy and cereal products (the corn being ground down on the hand-querns each squad of men had at its disposal, to produce bread, soup, and pasta-type dishes), with vegetables, nuts, oysters, mussels and whelks, fruit, fish and some meat; for the latter, evidence has survived in the form of animal bones recovered on excavations. The soldiers ate mutton and beef, bacon, even boar and deer, either boiled in bronze saucepans, or roasted on a spit. Wine was drunk, and beer.

Attitudes of mind are less easy to pinpoint. Seldom have we in Scotland the insights provided by papyri recovered from the dry sands of Egypt. Revelations about life at Vindolanda behind Hadrian's Wall, surviving on thin wooden writing-tablets preserved in damp conditions, are particularly informative: the food consumed, the requests written, hopes expressed and dashed. For Scotland we have as yet no specific written evidence of this sort – though the few graffiti show the potential for the recovery of some non-official corrective to the standard picture.

We can only guess at the general round of duties, though documents from other parts of the Roman Empire provide a helpful framework: the departure of patrols to the more remote valleys, anxiety for their safe return, standards seen gleaming in the distance presaging the return of the patrol to the delight of wives, children and ladies of the garrison-village; carousals in the tavern – most of the troops were Celts, with a love of beer rather than wine; quiet assignations in the side-alleys; business deals struck with local natives; the onset of winter with the roads blocked by snow – and no ploughs on Beattock summit or Carter Bar to keep them open; the news of an attack on an isolated fortlet beaten back or (much worse) successful; the death of an emperor, the swearing-in ceremony before the images of his successor, new messages and faces on the coins in the soldiers' pockets and purses; the essential sameness of frontier life for those who by choice or circumstances were destined to endure it; pay-days (every three months) accompanied by a parade; the arrival of a new centurion or prefect (higher officers enjoyed a mobility denied to 'other ranks'); new faces in the bath-house or at the brothel; the chance of special duty in another province, or beyond the frontier; limited leave (but how soldiers chose to spend it eludes us); hunting expeditions; death by disease or accident, after a quarrel, even by combat against the enemy; for the fortunate, survival to the date of discharge, often followed by voluntary settlement in close proximity to the frontier where ties were strongest and when a homeland left behind half a lifetime before was all but forgotten.

CHAPTER 9

The Impact of Rome

If we come to estimate the impact of the Romans on Scotland, we are bound to suppose that in the short term it was dramatic and devastating, at least for that part of the population which stood in the path of the invading army, or resisted its advance. The advent of the military forces of the Mediterranean world's current superpower cannot but have created a tremendous impression.

How much resistance was actually offered is less easy to estimate. Tacitus reports that Agricola was held up by bad weather in southern Scotland in AD 79, not by enemy opposition. Only north of the Forth–Clyde line did the army come under attack from the tribes of Caledonia. We know nothing from any literary source about the campaigns of Lollius Urbicus. The distance slabs sometimes depict scenes of combat, but these may be symbolic. Certainly the army of Severus had to fight, but he had penetrated beyond the floodtide of the Antonine advance into Caledonia where hostility to Rome could be expected.

Archaeologically the impact of the Roman advance is hard to pinpoint. If we suppose that the tribes resisted, we could look for signs of Roman retaliation or reduction of their strongholds. But even where some evidence of fires has been recovered during excavation, we cannot be certain that it resulted from Roman intervention rather than an accidental conflagration, or the inter-tribal warfare of which Tacitus speaks. One wall of the broch at Buchlyvie near Kippen fell or was pushed over, perhaps deliberately, at a date not long after AD 100–120. The event could belong to the time of the Roman advance in AD 142. The excavator of the broch at Leckie near Stirling believes that the site was stormed by a Roman force in AD 142, after which the structure was demolished almost to ground level.

It would have been normal Roman practice to seek the co-operation of the tribal nobility at the time of the invasions, or before, with offers of citizenship and imperial favour, in return for prompt declarations of allegiance and continued loyalty. Whether these methods were tried in Scotland, and what measure of success they enjoyed, we cannot say. The tribal area of the Damnonii was seemingly bisected by the Antonine Wall, with one part remaining inside the Empire and the other part beyond. The Votadini, it is alleged by scholars, enjoyed a favourable status: their hillfort at Traprain Law continued as a centre of population, or at least of power, with a surge of Roman luxury products attesting to its wealth and prosperity.

The sudden arrival of troops who needed to be clothed and fed would have a substantial effect on the local economy. At first the army brought up its own clothing, leather, shoes and crockery from the south, but it would be natural to suppose that more and more local produce would be purchased at the fort-gates, or by individual soldiers who wished to supplement rations and obtain the products of local craftsmanship.

We can also suppose some effect on the local environment. Road building required stone and gravel, with a strip of land cleared to either side to provide visibility and protect travellers from sudden attack. The construction of forts made an even greater impact: timber was required in large quantities, and turf had to be cut. It has been estimated that a fort of four acres would have needed 22,000 cubic feet of timber to construct its internal buildings, towers and gates. The construction of the Antonine Wall is estimated to have used up a corridor of turf 50m wide to both front and rear of the frontier line, assuming that suitable turf was available nearby. We have little enough secure information on the environment when the Romans arrived, but we should not suppose that it was entirely tree-covered, at least in the Lowlands. Recent botanical studies of the vicinity on the Antonine Wall suggest a landscape of heathland and grassland, with the woodland cut back for the pasturing of animals. Whether the Roman presence did much to alter the traditional way of life for the great mass of the population may be doubted. We should not suppose that the tribesmen exchanged their cloaks for togas or began to speak Latin. Certainly this was the sequence in other provinces; but we cannot document it for Scotland. In essence, for Scotland the periods of occupation were too short, though some beginnings of local government in the Roman manner, and the encouragement of chiefs to adopt a Roman lifestyle, could be supposed.

The Roman army had, however, no reason to suppose that its sojourn in Scotland, either in the later 1st century or mid-2nd century, would be brief. It was after all highly unusual for the Romans to withdraw from any territory overrun. But their withdrawal must certainly have shaken the confidence of native tribes and individuals who had sided too ostentatiously with the new masters. The decision to withdraw would have been followed by some demolition work. From Inchtuthil has come the famous hoard of almost one million unused nails, buried below the floor of the fortress workshop, where they remained hidden from human gaze (and the hands of the native population) until 1956 (Fig. 87). Samian pottery and glass vessels from the stores were tipped into the drains, and smashed underfoot. Timber-framed barracks were dismantled and burnt. The sequence is repeated at many forts where investigation allows a conclusion. At the close of the Antonine occupation, we know that at Bar Hill the headquarters building was carefully dismantled, with fitments and major structural timbers and stonework (column shafts and capitals) thrown into an adjacent well, a convenient repository.

It would not be unexpected if some pro-Roman elements among the native tribes migrated southwards with the troops, for fear of retaliation against them as collaborators. Readers may recall the confusion attending the final American withdrawal from Vietnam, when some local officials sought every means of accompanying the departing soldiers rather than face the wrath of their countrymen in a post-occupation society.

The longer-term effects of Roman occupation seem to have been limited. The sites of forts, stripped of re-usable materials, became overgrown and forgotten, except that place-name evidence can still provide clues: for example Kirkintilloch is originally the Gaelic Cairpentalloch, 'the fort at the end of the ridge'; Cramond is Caer Almond, 'the fort on the (river) Almond.' The road-system remained in use, until the cobbles wore away and the stones were dislodged; sometimes medieval hollow-ways followed the Roman route to one side. The English king Edward I marched northwards to Falkirk in 1298 by way of Dere Street, and in 1314 Robert Bruce before the battle at Bannockburn waited for the army of Edward II astride the Roman road northwards from Camelon towards Stirling.

It should not be imagined that the Roman presence in Scotland itself influenced the spread of Christianity – which came much later, with St. Ninian, St. Kentigern and St. Columba in the 5th and 6th centuries.

The Latin language and the classical tradition have been two factors in Scottish education, but the impulses were from the continent. Scots law is based directly (unlike English law) on the Roman system, but this has been a result of contacts with France and Italy during the Middle Ages and at the Renaissance, not from any memory of the Roman presence in Scotland itself.

There is a persistent Scottish tradition that Pontius Pilate, procurator (or, as we now know from an inscription, prefect) of Judaea at the time of the Crucifixion, was born at Fortingall in Perthshire, while his father was in Scotland as a Roman emissary at the court of a local king. However, the story seems to lack any solid foundation, even in the early chroniclers. Fortingall itself lies beyond any Roman sites as yet identified in Perthshire.

The conquest of Britain pulled the Romans further from their Mediterranean focus, to little clear advantage. If the modern Scot finds that London seems a long way from Edinburgh, and even further from the Highlands, let him consider the distance beween Scotland and Rome, in an age of slow communications. Instead of bemoaning the fate of Rome's Scottish endeavours, we should be surprised that they were ever contemplated at all. The modern nationalist viewpoint makes much of the Romans' failure in Scotland, seeing in their withdrawals and in the difficulties encountered evidence of the bravery and resourcefulness of the muscular Caledonians in the face of the imperialist aggressor. Their failure (if failure it was – and this implies that the Romans wanted more of Scotland and could not get it) should be ascribed less to the whims of particular emperors, more to the difficult terrain and harsh climate and in general to the pointlessness of further expenditures of men and material to secure progressively poorer land, with little obvious economic return. Britain was always a fringe province of the Roman Empire.

Part 2

Visiting Scotland's Roman Remains

Introduction

The following pages are designed to provide the visitor, whether by car or on foot, with a guide to the visible testimony to the Roman period in Scotland's past. The three main sections describe (1) Roman remains south of the Antonine Wall, from south to north; (2) the Antonine Wall itself, from east to west; and (3) Scotland north of the Antonine Wall, from south to north. If this sequence seems hard on those who, like the writer, live in the densest area of modern population in Scotland, the Glasgow conurbation, or those who live in the North-East, it can be pointed out that the Romans entered Scotland from the south, and it seems wisest to discover Scotland from the same direction as they did. In general each sub-section within the itineraries can be followed in a day or two of reasonable length by car. Obviously the cyclist or walker (who regrettably in these days is presumed to be in a minority) will take longer over the itineraries – by no means a bad thing. Finding a site and inspecting the surviving remains often take longer than expected, and advance preparation with suitable maps will save time on the day. Solid footwear and waterproof clothing against adverse weather conditions are always advisable, as some visits involve crossing mist-covered moorland and bog, forestry plantations or streams in full torrent. There is no space here to describe hotels or hostelries along the routes followed, which the writer might wish to recommend or condemn from his own experience.

Visitors should recall that, while in Scotland there is no law of trespass as such, all land belongs to someone, and it is only sensible and courteous to enquire, even in this age of equality, at a nearby farmhouse or cottage to see if the owner is agreeable. It is not the aim of this guide to alienate landowners and farmers who have in the past been amenable to archaeological exploration and endeavour.

All but a few Roman sites in Scotland are scheduled under the Ancient Monuments Act (1979), and several forts and lengths of the Antonine Wall are 'guardianship monuments' in the care of the Secretary of State for Scotland – the Scottish equivalent of the protection formerly accorded in England by the Department of the Environment, and now by the Historic Buildings and Monuments Commission (English

Heritage). In the following pages the abbreviation AM = ancient monument.

An attempt has been made in the following pages to direct the visitor to those Roman sites in Scotland where something meaningful survives above ground. These sites are printed in bold type. Sites of some distinction in the Scottish context are marked by a single asterisk, and those of outstanding merit and impressiveness by two asterisks. The purpose of such grading is to direct the visitor, with a minimum of time, to see the best remains. All Roman sites known in Scotland to the end of 1985 are marked on the accompanying maps (except for the construction camps along the Antonine Wall), though only those discussed in the following pages are individually named. For further information the reader is referred to the current fourth or forthcoming fifth edition of the Ordnance Survey *Map of Roman Britain*. Details on access are generally given only for those sites where there is something definite to see. In general the accompanying Figures show only those Roman roads confirmed by the Ordnance Survey; other stretches tentatively identified over the years are noted annually in *Discovery and Excavation in Scotland*.

Ideally the visitor should aim to carry Ordnance Survey 1:50,000 (or one-inch) maps of a particular area, and the check-list below (at p. 178) provides a six-figure NGR (National Grid Reference) for all sites mentioned. An AA or RAC handbook will not suffice. The old OS quarter-inch maps which show clearly mountains, river valleys and other important geographical features may provide a useful insight into *why* Roman roads and installations are placed in particular localities, so that the whole network of sites should begin to make more sense. For the Antonine Wall the special Ordnance Survey historical map (HMSO 1969) is essential.

The reader will find below no references to 'opening hours' of the sites described. Most lie in open farmland, and even those which are in government care can be visited at will, without charge.

With a single exception all the sites mentioned were visited (or revisited) by the author in 1984–85. Details on access were noted then, but as time passes, sites become overgrown, fences are erected or pulled down, signposts and landmarks fall victim to 'agricultural improvement' and the pace of development. The author would be glad to know of changes in access routes, of better methods of approach to the sites mentioned, or of difficulties encountered.

CHAPTER 10

Scotland South of the Antonine Wall

A. Annandale

For the Romans, as for later invaders and the modern traveller, the route to the North started at Carlisle, and led to the Dumfriesshire Esk at Netherby (where there was a fort in the grounds of Netherby House) and then into Annandale. The first major Roman site within the modern political boundaries of Scotland was at **Birrens***. Turn off the A74 at Ecclefechan; then take the B725 for Middlebie. Turn sharp right in Middlebie itself, and just after the road passes between two cottages but before it crosses a hump-backed bridge, park on the left at the track for Satur farm, opposite a dilapidated stile which leads to the fort-site.) The fort was first built in the Flavian period, and several times reconstructed and enlarged in the Hadrianic and Antonine periods, and held up to about AD 180. The visible ramparts, belonging to the Antonine fort, stand to a height of 1m; on the N side of the fort are six ditches, which survive as faint hollows. The S end of the fort has been eroded by the adjacent stream. No trace can be seen of any internal buildings, which were completely excavated in 1895, with further work carried out in 1937–38 and 1962–69. Numerous altars and sculptured reliefs (now in Dumfries or Edinburgh) have been found at Birrens over the centuries, and during the 1895 excavations; many testify to the activities of the Second Cohort of Tungrians, the garrison from AD 158 till the abandonment of the fort.

Some 4km to the NW of Birrens rises the imposing eminence of **Burnswark Hill**,** its summit occupied by an Iron Age fort where occupation began in the 7th century BC. On the lower slopes to both N and S are Roman camps, evidently designed to house a force besieging the native fort. (From Birrens return to Middlebie and take the B725 W towards Ecclefachan; shortly before the road crosses the railway line and then the A74, turn sharp right. Soon after, Burnswark Hill with a plantation below its E peak comes into view; park at a road junction just before a sign for Burnswark farm. Take

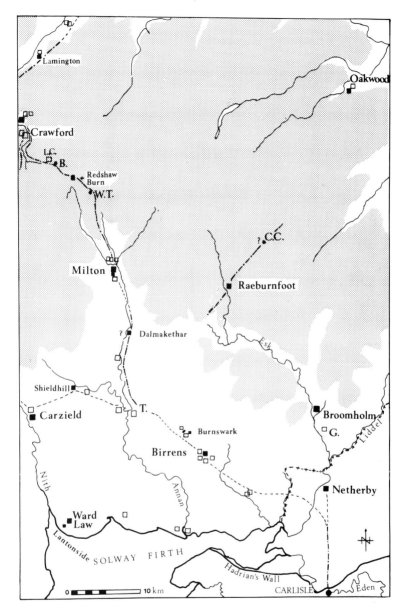

36. **Annandale and Eskdale**. Note: B. = Beattock Summit, C.C. = Craik Cross Hill, G. = Gilnockie, L.C. = Little Clyde, T. = Torwood, W.T. = White Type.

37. Birrens, Dumfriesshire: aerial view of the Antonine fort from the SE. (Photo: Ministry of Defence, British Crown Copyright Reserved.)

38. Statuette of Brigantia, tutelary goddess of the Brigantes tribe of northern England; from Birrens, Dumfriesshire. (Photo: National Museums of Scotland.) Brigantia has been given the attributes of several classical goddesses. She wears a turreted crown, symbolising her protective role, the weapons and gorgon-medallion of the goddess Minerva, the wings of Victory and the globe and navel-stone (bottom left) of Celestial Juno. This statuette is an excellent example of the amalgamation of attributes so common in Roman religion (see above, p. 48).

39. **Altar to Disciplina**, erected by the Second Cohort of Tungrians; from Birrens, Dumfriesshire. (Photo: National Museums of Scotland.) See also p. 158.

40. **Burnswark, Dumfriesshire**: aerial view showing the 'siege-camp' S of the hillfort. (Photo: Cambridge University Committee for Aerial Photography.)

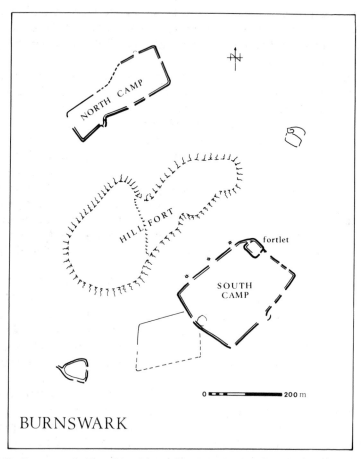

BURNSWARK

41. Burnswark, Dumfriesshire (after Jobey), showing the hillfort, with Roman 'siege-camps' to N and S (the latter overlying a fortlet), and other earthworks nearby of uncertain date.

the rough track through the trees, left of this sign, to reach the summit.) The camps are best viewed from the hilltop. That on the S flank is the better preserved: the camp-rampart facing the hill is interrupted by three entrances, in front of which are three circular platforms 20m across (known in local legend as the Three Brethren), probably intended as emplacements for artillery. The S camp incorporates within its NE corner a fortlet of Antonine date which predates it. The camp on the N side of the Hill (best seen from its E summit) is less well preserved, but much of its somewhat irregular outline is clear. Excavation on the hilltop in 1898 and in the later 1960s revealed catapult balls and sling-bullets evidently propelled into the fort from the Roman camps below.

At first sight Burnswark is Scotland's Masada, but whether it witnessed a great siege, heroic defence and final sacrifice has been doubted. There are no continuous siege-lines round the Hill, and excavation on the summit in 1966–68 suggested that the defences were long disused when Roman missiles were directed into the interior. It is possible therefore that the camps, which apparently contained stone buildings and showed other signs of careful construction and extended occupation, served as a training area for troops, perhaps from Hadrian's Wall or from Birrens, and provided an opportunity for peacetime artillery practice and the mock-storming of hillforts. Whatever explanation is preferred, the view from Burnswark Hill to the camps is an evocative reminder of the strength and discipline of the Roman army.

From Netherby a branch road evidently continued up the Esk. The ramparts of one camp along this route can be seen at **Gilnockie**. (From the A7 2km N of Canonbie, turn right on to the A720, then left on to a minor road signposted Claygate 1; then follow the B6318 N for 600m, past a house on the left; at the next stretch of woodland, take a track leftwards beside the trees. After 100m a low bank with accompanying ditch is in view on the left side of the track). This is the E rampart of a 25-acre (10 ha.) camp. This rampart can be followed to the SE corner of the camp, then right into woodland; it survives as a low-spread bank 4m wide and 0.5m high. Just before the rampart enters the woodland, there is a gateway 20m wide defended by a traverse. Within the wood the rampart can be followed for 350m; there is a second gateway, also defended by a traverse; the rampart continues as a bracken-covered mound as far as the end of the woodland, where the site of the SW corner of the camp is damaged by a now disused railway.

Further N along the Esk is a fort of 4.5 acres (1.8 ha.) at **Broomholm**, partly constructed on top of a native enclosure. The fort was first built in the Flavian period. Later, perhaps under Hadrian, the fort was replaced by a fortlet, as an outpost for Hadrian's Wall. Occupation of the fortlet ended in destruction, followed by native re-use of the site. (Continue from Gilnockie along the B6318 till a stone-built viaduct comes into view; the fort lies on the hill beyond. Cross

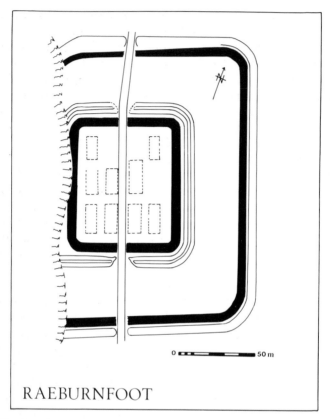

RAEBURNFOOT

42. **Raeburnfoot, Dumfriesshire**: ground-plan of the Antonine fort and outer enclosure (after Robertson).

the Tarras Water on foot using the viaduct, then veer to the right to reach the hilltop along a line of telegraph poles; stop at the second pole.) Three ditches are visible here, defending the SW corner of the annexe of the Flavian fort, with a causeway across the ditches to reach a gate in the S side. A single ditch can be followed uphill along the fort's W side. On the hilltop, beyond a modern track defined by bankings, is a ditch on the N side of the fort, with a break for the N gate. Some way down the forward slope is a second ditch. Nothing is visible of the Hadrianic fortlet.

North of Birrens itself the main road through Annandale continued NW well to the E of the river to Torwood near Lockerbie where the road splits, one arm going N up the valley of the Annan, the other reaching W towards the Nith (below, p. 84). There was a camp at Torwood itself, of which one rampart, on the W side, is faintly traceable. Another road seems likely to have branched off the Annandale route hereabouts, following the modern B723, along the Dryfe Water to the Esk at **Raeburnfoot**, where a small fort of Antonine date, defended by a double ditch, and containing nine or more rectangular buildings (perhaps stores), was subsequently enclosed within a substantial outer work and single ditch, the latter partly eroded on the W side by the Esk. (At Eskdalemuir, watch for a minor road leaving the B709 just before it crosses to the W bank of the White Esk; follow the minor road towards a farm, then veer left behind a wood, and follow the track for 1.3km to Raeburnfoot Farm. The outlines of the fort can be seen on high ground to the left). First the visitor will cross the ditch and bank of the outer enclosure, then the ditches and rampart of the fort itself, which are particularly impressive on the S and N sides where the ditch is 1m deep.

The Roman road beyond Raeburnfoot to the NE can be followed on the ground to the Borthwick Water, a tributary of the Teviot. (Drive beyond Raeburnfoot farm to Mid Raeburn; stop at a gate just before a bridge leading to the farm, pass through it and follow a track along the edge of some forestry; the Roman road from Raeburnfoot crosses this track from right to left at a firebreak, and continues uphill. The low mound of the road can now be followed along the firebreak for 6km over a sequence of hilltops, finally to reach Craik Cross Hill on the Dumfriesshire/Roxburghshire border, from which fine views are to be had on a clear day towards the Eildon Hills above Melrose.) The Roman road survives as a low mound, sometimes with cuttings to ease the gradients. On the summit of **Craik Cross Hill**, immediately N of the Roman road, and just before a boundary fence, is a circular mound, perhaps to be identified as a Roman watch-tower. (A full day is necessary for the walk from Raeburnfoot and back; the site can also be reached from the NE, from Craik village; see OS 1:50,000 sheet for details of route.) Limited excavation in 1946 identified a turf-built rampart and single ditch, but no foundations for timber or other buildings were noted on the interior, nor were any small finds recovered; so that the Roman dating is not secure. Further NE along this road, at Milsington, on the Borthwick Water, one leg of a bronze statue, of a man on horseback, perhaps loot from some fort or a town in the South, was found in 1820.

The Annandale road itself continued N along the E bank of the river. At **Dalmakethar** E of Johnstonebridge, on high ground with good views along the river valley, is a square enclosure, possibly but not certainly a Roman fortlet, with a single entrance facing the Roman road. (Leave the A74 at the Dinwoodie Lodge Hotel, going N on a minor road; c. 400m after the side track to Dalmakethar farm, park on the left and walk uphill, on the left of the road, until the ridge is reached.) The ramparts stand to a height of 1m. The results of excavation in 1939 were inconclusive as to the date and function of the site.

At **Milton** 8km further N there was a notable complex of Roman sites originally surveyed by General Roy and excavated between 1938 and 1950. Here, at the N edge of a prominent ridge overlooking the Annan, was a fort of the Flavian period overlying a native enclosure. This was replaced in the Antonine age by a fortlet enclosing an area of 44 × 28m. (Turn left off the A74 by signs for the A701 to Dumfries, then left to pass below the dual carriageway, and immediately right on to a minor road. Milton farm is the second building on the left. Ask there for permission to proceed, and drive through the farm to a gate across the track. Park here and follow a fence line to the left uphill to the top of the ridge. Look left to see the standing remains of the Antonine fortlet (see Fig. 19) whose rampart survives to a height of 1.2m within an enclosing ditch.) North of Milton there are three camps and a possible fortlet at Beattock village. Evidently there was a staging post here for traffic before it began ascending to Beattock summit; we could also suspect some Roman movement eastwards from Beattock towards the Ettrick Water. To the N of Beattock the Roman road rises over moorland, and a worthwhile stretch can be viewed at **'Gilbert's Rig'**. (Take the A701 N from Moffat, then go left on to the B719 (signposted Abington); after c. 400m stop at a 'layby' on the right beside a swift-flowing burn; on the opposite side of the road, some of the bottoming from the Roman road is visible in a modern embankment; from the layby cross the burn, passing to the right of an old sheep-pen.) Here the road, with its cambered surface, is in view, with shallow cuttings to improve the gradient on the slope, and numerous quarry pits especially on the left side as the road ascends to the hillock known as Gilbert's Rig.

As the road continues to rise, there is a probable watch-tower close by its course at **White Type**. (On the A701 N of Moffat, park at Auldhousehill bridge, beside a two-storeyed concrete building; go left through a farm gate 100m ahead (the fence is electrified). Some 80m into the field, the Roman road crosses the track going half-right towards a cutting. Follow the Roman road as it curves to the left to reach a small stream; here a modern track, one of many hereabouts, goes off to the right; continue straight ahead and after the road passes through a cutting, watch for hillocks on the left. The watch-tower occupies one of these, with its shallow circular ditch interrupted by a causeway towards the road. The site is easy to miss; if you reach a forestry plantation, or an area of flat marshland, you have gone too far.)

Beyond White Type was a fortlet, at **Redshaw Burn★**, first seen from the air in 1939, close to the watershed between the valleys of the Annan, Clyde and Tweed. (Take the B719 from Moffat to its junction with the A74, then go N past the 'Strathclyde Region' sign, to a railway bridge; a minor road just S of the bridge, more easily accessible for those travelling S, leads to Nether Howecleugh farm; do not enter the walled garden of the farm, but continue along the track to a gate; park here and take a track uphill for 2km into some forestry; twice keep to the right where the track splits, and soon after it crosses the headwaters of the Redshaw Burn, here contained in a pipe, veer to the right towards some open ground; the fortlet lies 100m ahead, resting against the steep bank down to the Burn.) The fortlet, which measures c. 20m E–W by 17.5m N–S, is enclosed by a rampart and by a double ditch. In the N side of the fortlet facing the road was a single gate, defended by a long stretch of ditch enclosing a small annexe. (This outer ditch is the feature the visitor will encounter first.) The Roman road, passing in front of the fortlet, lies just clear of the forestry. Some 3.5km N is another watch-tower, called Beattock Summit, on a steep slope beside the Roman road; first seen from the air, it was established as Roman in 1966. The circular ditch and external bank once stood out clearly, but the site is now destroyed by afforestation. It is clear that close surveillance was maintained along this particularly difficult stretch of road.

A further 500m N at **Little Clyde** farm is a marching camp of 31 acres (12.7 ha.) immediately beside the Roman road. The farm sits in the middle of the camp whose ramparts stand to a height of up to 0.7m. (Reached from the S-bound carriageway of the A74, on a minor track signposted 'Little Clyde'; go uphill for 30m behind the farm, keeping to the left of a turbulent stream, to see the camp's N rampart, which can be followed both W and E for 200m to the NW and NE corners.) In the late 18th century a marble head of a Roman emperor or general, slightly larger than lifesize, broken off a statue, was found at Hawkshead, close to the source of the Tweed, 10km NE from Little Clyde; it may have been loot from a Roman site.

B. Nithsdale

An alternative route for the Romans (and for the modern traveller) from Carlisle to the Clyde was via the valley of the Nith. This road left the Annandale route at Torwood (above, p. 80), and made for **Dalswinton**, where there was a large fort of the Flavian era, excavated in 1939 and shown to have an area of about 6.4 acres (2.59 ha.) over the ramparts, with accommodation for a cavalry unit. (From the A76 go right at Auldgirth on to a minor road; after 3km turn S on to a farm track signposted Dalswinton. Cross the low-lying ground, noticing a dip in the slope opposite: this marks the N defences of the fort close to the NE corner; park where the road splits; the T-junction lies approximately on the site of the E gate of the fort.) There were in fact two forts at Dalswinton: the second, much larger, on low ground beside the Nith at Bankfoot farm, seems likely to have been the earlier of the two, and may belong to the period of Agricola's active campaigning. Other Roman camps and installations, including a watchtower, have been tentatively identified nearby from the air.

In the Antonine period, Dalswinton was replaced as the likely nodal point of Roman activity in Nithsdale by a new fort at **Carzield**, 5km to the S. (Continue S from Dalswinton on the minor road, then right at the signpost for Carzield; park in the middle of the hamlet at the lodge-house, which is almost at the centre of the fort; to see the rampart and ditches on the E side retrace steps for 100m along the road until the dip of the ditch comes into view on the left beside farm buildings.) The modern roads still pass out of the fort more or less on the sites of the four gateways. A stone-built cavalry barracks, excavated in 1939, is marked today by a long mound in the SE quarter of the fort. (Walk S from the Lodge.) The rampart and ditches are visible along the fort's S side (E of the road) and at the SE corner. W of the fort, the ground drops away steeply to the floodplain of the Nith. Finds from some of the fort's rubbish-pits, dug out in 1967–68, can be seen in Dumfries Museum.

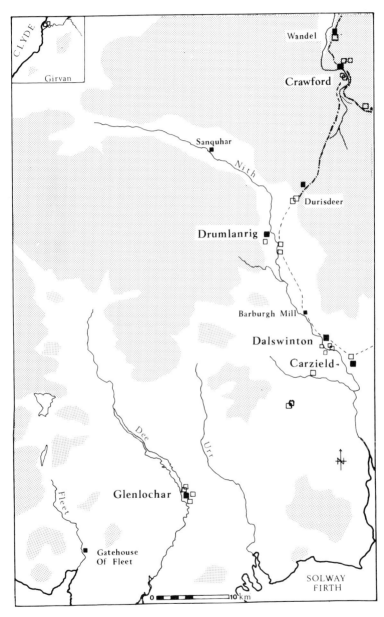

43. **Nithsdale and Kirkcudbright.**

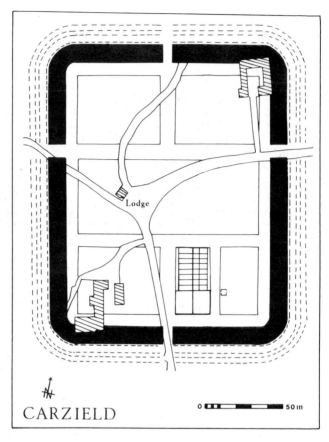

44. Carzield, Dumfriesshire. Ground-plan of Antonine fort (after Birley and Richmond).

Northwards from Carzield, the road was protected in the Antonine period by a fortlet at Barburgh Mill on a high plateau above the east bank of the Nith (Fig. 19). The site is now quarried away, but comprehensive excavation in 1971 revealed two timber-framed buildings, sufficient to house a century of 80 men, perhaps outstationed from Carzield. At Carronbridge aerial photography long ago revealed a complex of sites, including a temporary camp, but other features are better placed in the Iron Age or Mediaeval periods. Recently (in the summer of 1984) a small fort of some 3 acres has been found from the air on the other, W side of the Nith, hard by the Castle of **Drumlanrig**.

45. **Durisdeer, Dumfriesshire**: Antonine fortlet, seen from the E, looking down into the valley of the Nith. (Photo: L. Keppie.)

(The Castle is signposted from the A76 during the summer.) The fort-platform can easily be seen on the ground, 400m SE of the Castle. (From the adventure woodland walk S to the edge of the plateau, overlooking the floodplain of the Nith.) The S rampart stands to a height of 0.4m just back from the escarpment, and the hollow of a ditch can be seen at the SW corner; an annexe has also been plotted, as has a marching camp, and Antonine pottery has been found close by. This fort surely points to the existence of a road, its course as yet undetected, following the Nith to the NW towards Kilmarnock and the Ayrshire plain; a fortlet is now reported on this route at Sanquhar.

The known road veers away NE, and where it rises to enter the pass above the village of **Durisdeer★★**, there is a magnificently preserved fortlet. (Turn off the A702 4km N of Carronbridge, along a minor road – overlying the Roman road – into Durisdeer village; park at the church and take a track on its right N for c. 800m; pass through a field gate on the left on to a farm track, and shortly after crossing a stream the fortlet should be in full view straight ahead.) The fortlet was defended by a rampart of turf now standing 1.2m high, within a single ditch. These defences present a formidable obstacle still, with a height-difference of some 4m between the bottom of the ditch and the top of the rampart. The gate was to the NE (facing into the pass), and was defended by a traverse ditch and rampart – the former is still visible, c. 11m long and 0.3m deep. Excavation in 1938 revealed two timber-built structures in the interior, and evidence of two phases of occupation. The road climbs to enter the pass, to the left of the Kirk Burn and subsequently the Potrail Water. (A walk of 6km, much recommended.) At first the course of the road is marked by a modern track, but where the latter peters out it can be detected by terracings as it continues uphill. (Keep to the left of the field dyke.) Joined again by a modern track, it curves left round the Well Hill, till it descends towards the modern A702. Where the Roman road approaches the modern highway (which has here followed the lower, and even more spectacular, Dalveen Pass), it survives as a fine cambered mound, which continues across the modern road for 500m before veering right and descending towards Over Fingland farm. The Roman road now ran on NE (its course may be detected from time to time 200m N of the line of the A702, especially beyond Glenochar farm), until it eventually joined the Annandale route at Crawford (below, p. 89).

Roman incursions along the Scottish coastline of the Solway Firth, or perhaps incursions up the river valleys from the Firth, are demonstrated by a camp at either side of the mouth of the River Annan and another further W (at Ruthwell). Close by the mouth of the Nith is a fort at **Ward Law** astride a saddleback ridge which stands out from afar. (Off the B725 S of Dumfries close to Caerlaverock Castle. Best reached from a rough farm-track going uphill at the sign for Blackshaw; continue uphill behind the farm, keeping to the right of a circular plantation of trees at the S end of the ridge.) The climb is very worthwhile for views over the Solway, but the Roman fort-ramparts may prove difficult to detect if the crop is high; the fort's E rampart can be seen as a dip in the field about two-thirds up the slope. Excavation in 1939 and 1949–50 revealed that the fort had an area of 6.9 acres (2.8 ha.); the enclosing ditch was partly rock-cut. No small finds were made, so that the date of the fort is uncertain. Its large size may argue for the Flavian period. The trees at the end of the ridge conceal the double ramparts of an Iron Age hillfort, to which the Roman fort was apparently linked by a ditch. On lower ground to the SW, immediately behind the sand-flats at the mouth of the Nith, is a fortlet, at Lantonside, recently located from the air (Fig. 36).

A route SW from Dalswinton led towards a major concentration of installations at **Glenlochar** on the Kirkcudbrightshire Dee where a large fort of some 9 acres (3.6 ha.), occupied in both Flavian and Antonine periods, is hedged about with at least five camps. Obviously, substantial Roman forces passed this way on several occasions. (On the A713, 3km N of Castle Douglas, turn left on to the B795; the fort lies at a group of cottages just before the river.) The fort-platform can be made out, and the W rampart (on the left of the road just beyond the cottages) survives as a low mound 0.3m high with a causeway across the ditches. A stretch of ditch at the NW corner of the site (in the field opposite the cottages), is particularly impressive (Fig. 34). At Gatehouse of Fleet, a fortlet was located from the air in 1949, and excavated in 1960–61. It lay on high ground overlooking the course of the Water of Fleet, with good views N up the river valley. It is difficult to suppose that this was the terminal site for any Roman road along the coast of Galloway, and indeed a stretch of roadway running W from the fortlet towards the river was identified from the air and recently tested on the ground by Professor St. Joseph. We can look in the future for sites to be discovered at Newton Stewart and at or near Stranraer, where Loch Ryan provides a fine natural harbour.

C. Clydesdale

At **Crawford** village, now bypassed by the A74, a small fort, placed at the confluence between the Clyde and the Camps Water, guarded the junction of the Annandale and the Nithsdale Roman roads. Initially discovered from the air in 1938 and confirmed as Roman by trial excavation, the fort was extensively excavated in 1961–66 when occupation in both Flavian and Antonine periods was established, with ramparts of turf and internal buildings of timber. (Turn off the A74 for Crawford village; at the N end of the main street, turn right at a monument to cross the railway, immediately left then right once more at a T-junction; park at or before a cottage on the right near the ruins of Castle Crawford. The fort lies in the field opposite.) Little can be made out except that the N and W ramparts are vaguely discernible in pasture, as are the SW, NW and NE corners (go to the second pair of trees, directly opposite the cottage, to see the line of the W rampart). At Crawford the Roman road left the valley of the Clyde, to climb through the hills E of the river, on a more direct route towards Abington than that followed today by the A74. (From the fort, head towards the hills, then go right, along the fence, to a group of trees. Now go uphill for 400m. The road may prove difficult to detect.) It soon passes through a cutting, and turns sharp right to follow a level

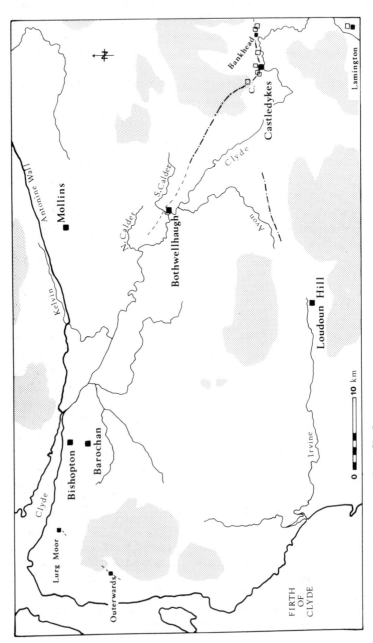

46. **The Clyde Valley**. Note: C. = Cleghorn.

terrace, becoming more and more impressive as it works its way round
the lower slope of **Raggengill Hill**; it can now be followed easily for
1.5km, though the course is occasionally interrupted by the metalled
track of an 18th century successor. The road continues towards
Abington with the Raggengill Burn below, and the ramparts of an
Iron Age fort on Arbory Hill above. At Wandel, 4km N of Abington,
is a probable fortlet (similar in size to Redshaw Burn) and a temporary
camp. At nearby Lamington a camp has been observed together with
another possible fortlet. The Roman road continued NE past Biggar,
crossing the Tweeddale road (below, p. 107) at Melbourne (where the
A702 from the S still crosses the A721), and continued NE along the S
flank of the Pentlands, and latterly along the left bank of the North
Esk to link up with the Lauderdale road (below, p. 110). Claims have
been made from time to time for a fort at Biggar, and long ago
Alexander Gordon referred to an enclosure 'similar to Ardoch' at
Carlops; recently a sequence of camps has been identified from the air
along this route. Surprisingly there is as yet no direct link confirmed
from Crawford (or Lamington) to the important fort at Castledykes
(below), for example along the Clyde itself past Thankerton on the
line of the A73 and the railway, though such a route is reported by the
antiquarian writers.

   The fort at **Castledykes** is situated above the Clyde where the hills
have opened out to leave a wide stretch of flat land fringed by the
western Pentlands and Tinto Hill. (On the A70 E of Lanark; 3km N of
Hyndford Bridge turn right at a line of prefabricated houses; follow
the farm-track signposted to Corbiehall, and where the road bends to
the left, go straight on, through a farm gate; 200m further on, the
rising ground marks the beginning of the fort-platform.) The limits of
the fort are easily made out on all sides, especially on the S where the
ground drops away towards the floodplain of the Clyde. (It should be
remembered that the course of the Clyde has changed over the
centuries and that in Roman times it probably flowed immediately
below the fort.) The track passes through the fort's W gate on a slight
causeway, with the ditch visible to either side and as a matching
hollow in the nearby field-fence to the S. Continue on the track,
through another gate, beyond which a substantial mound, standing
on either side of the track to a height of 1.5m, represents the E
rampart. Excavation between 1937 and 1955 established that the fort,
which faced S towards the Clyde, was occupied in both the Flavian
and Antonine periods. The central buildings were probably of timber

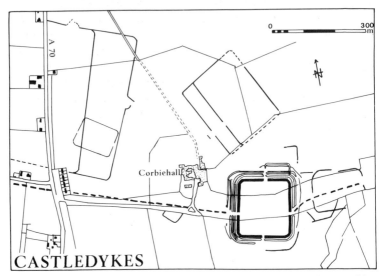

47. **Castledykes, Lanarkshire**: ground-plan of the fort and nearby marching camps (after RCAHMS).

in the Flavian period but certainly of stone in the Antonine; a squared building-block, having one face dressed to receive an inscription, and decorated with the incised figure of a capricorn, testifies to construction work by men of the Second Legion, which used the capricorn as one of its emblems. To the N and W of the fort were half a dozen temporary camps, for troops in transit. Clearly this was an important staging post, as was its nearby Victorian equivalent, Carstairs railway junction.

What seems to be the course of a Roman road running NW into Clydesdale can be seen just W of Castledykes fort, where it survives in a narrow strip of woodland N of the farm access road. Soon after, the road passes a well-preserved camp of 46 acres (18.9 ha.) at **Cleghorn** surveyed by William Roy in 1764, parts of whose N and E sides survive impressively in a forestry plantation. (Best reached from the A706 out of Lanark; soon after a level-crossing, take a minor road N opposite a restaurant and caravan park towards some woodland; park in a new picnic area on the right and walk W along the minor road until it bends slightly to the left; there, on the right-hand side, some 20m further on, the camp's N rampart can be seen stretching into the plantation, called Camp Wood, along a cleared strip.) The rampart can be followed on foot for 350m to its NE corner, with the ditch on the left, now serving as a drainage channel. At the corner, the rampart turns sharply to the right and can be followed with increasing difficulty (modern plantation bankings confuse the Roman line) towards the A706. There were two entrances in the N side of the camp, both marked by traverses lying 10m beyond the rampart. The first lies just 40m into the plantation beyond the minor road; it can be reached by the intrepid visitor. The second lies 150m further on, in an area left clear in the plantation.

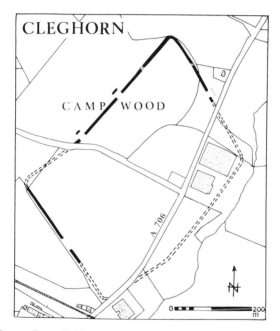

48. **Cleghorn, Lanarkshire**: ground-plan of the marching camp (after RCAHMS).

The Roman road now continues NW well above the right bank of the Clyde. The best visible stretch is at **Collielaw Wood**. (Continue along the minor road N from Cleghorn past woodland on the left; just short of Collielaw farm, walk left along the line of a double wire fence on the N side of the woodland, almost to the edge of the wood, where a cambered mound with side-ditches comes into view.) Its course is visible running both N towards Collielaw farm and S into the wood.

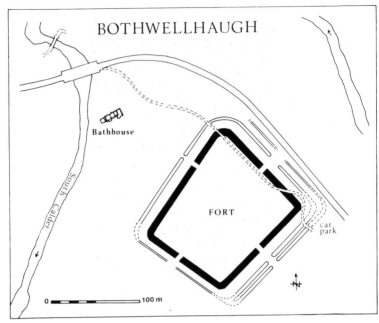

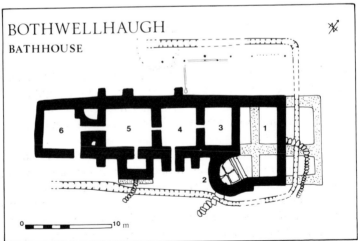

49. Bothwellhaugh, Lanarkshire. Top: fort and bathhouse (after RCAHMS). Bottom: bathhouse (after Keppie). Note: 1 = cold room, 2 = cold plunge bath, 3–4 = warm rooms, 5 = hot room, 6 = main furnace. Stippling indicates foundations for walling which was never completed.

50. **Bothwellhaugh**: the bathhouse, with cold plunge in foreground. (Photo: L. Keppie.)

Recent excavation here has confirmed the presence of the metalled road scarcely 5cms below the modern surface. The road continues N on high ground until it is swallowed up in the modern towns of Wishaw and Motherwell, where its alignment is preserved for a while by the modern A721.

North of Motherwell, within the grounds of Strathclyde Country Park, on high ground above the (former) junction between the Clyde and the South Calder Water, there was a fort of 4.1 acres (1.65 ha.) known today as **Bothwellhaugh★**. (From the M74, take the exit to Motherwell, A723; or the exit to Bothwell, A725; look for signs to Strathclyde Country Park. Within the Park, drive to the modern bridge across a small river, the South Calder Water. Park *off* the road in a picnic-area S of the river; the fort-site lies immediately to the N of the car park.) First reported in the 1790s, the fort was excavated in 1938–39 and in 1967–68. Only the SE rampart is easily picked out today on rough ground immediately N of the picnic area, where it stands to a height of 1.2m; the modern footpath leading downhill

51. **Bothwellhaugh**: floral drain-cover in centre of cold-room floor of the bathhouse. (Photo: W. A. C. Sharp; scale in inches.)

almost immediately crosses the fort's SE corner, with the embankment on the right representing what survives of the fort's NE rampart. The site offers splendid views up and down the Clyde valley. Below the fort, beside the South Calder, the fort-bathhouse was accidentally discovered in 1973 during the construction of Strathclyde Country Park, and excavated in 1975–76 in anticipation of flooding from the adjoining artificial loch, which now lies between the fort and the Clyde itself. (Continue down the footpath almost to the river.) In 1979–81 the remains were re-excavated, dismantled and rebuilt on the same site at a higher level, safe from the encroaching waters. The bathhouse was a finely constructed sandstone building, about 30 by 10m, with a cold room at the E end (nearest the fort). In the centre of the cold room floor was a slab carved with a floral design, to serve as a 'drain cover' (the original slab is in the Hunterian Museum, with a replica to be placed *in situ*). Opening off the cold room was a semicircular cold-plunge bath, and a sequence of heated rooms provided with underfloor hypocausts. At the W end of the building, adjacent to the South Calder, was a furnace room. An information board supplies useful details. Close by is an attractive hump-backed bridge, known locally as the Roman Bridge; it was probably built towards the end of the 15th century.

Beyond Bothwell the Roman road ran through Uddingston to Mount Vernon; some camps and even a fortlet might be looked for at the crossing of the North Calder Water, but the ground has been built over, or much disturbed. The course of the road through Glasgow itself is lost. We could suppose that it was heading for the W terminus of the Antonine Wall at Old Kilpatrick or for the fort at Balmuildy on the River Kelvin (below, p. 134). On high ground at Yorkhill in Glasgow, where the Kelvin meets the Clyde, Roman material of the Antonine period, including a coin and some pottery, was found long ago, but it has usually been thought to indicate a native homestead occupied in the Roman period. But the site would be ideal for an intermediate fort or fortlet between Bothwellhaugh and Old Kilpatrick.

To the E of Glasgow, at Mollins farm close to the modern A80 (Glasgow–Stirling road) on the Luggie Water, a small fort was unexpectedly revealed from the air in 1977; it was about one acre (0.4 ha.) in size with an annexe to the W. Trial excavation in 1977–78 established a Flavian date, so that Mollins may have been one of the garrison-posts which Tacitus tells us were constructed along the Forth–Clyde isthmus by Agricola in AD 80.

Another Flavian site, perhaps also to be linked to Agricola's work in AD 80, is at Barochan Hill (2km N of Houston in Renfrewshire, within a private estate). The fort was first seen from the air in 1953; excavation in 1972 and in 1984–85 established the position of two gateways and the alignment of internal buildings. The fort, of about 3.5 acres (1.4 ha.), with an annexe to the E, had wide views in all directions, though the site lies too far S of the Clyde to have exercised direct control over movements on or across the river. In the Antonine period, Barochan was not reoccupied, but its place was taken by a 4.9 acre (2.04 ha.) fort at Bishopton, on a plateau directly overlooking the Clyde, the lowest fordable point on the river's course at Dumbuck, and (on its further bank) the hillfort on Dumbarton Rock which was certainly occupied in the early centuries AD, and later became the capital of the Dark Age British kingdom of Strathclyde. Bishopton fort was located from the air in 1949 and extensively excavated in 1950–54. Nothing meaningful is visible today, but the visitor cannot fail to be impressed by the wide views over the Clyde estuary. (To appreciate the fort's position, take a minor road to the left of the A8 going W out of Bishopton village; after 1.5km, where the road begins to descend, and the Clyde comes into view, there is an old metal farm-tank sitting a little to the right of the road. The fort lies mainly in the field on the other side of the road.)

Close Roman surveillance over the Firth of Clyde can be assumed, with a sequence of watch-towers and fortlets along the S bank of the river. In 1952 aerial reconnaisance revealed a fortlet on **Lurg Moor*** above Greenock, with magnificent views towards the Gare Loch, the Holy Loch, and Loch Long. (In Greenock, travelling W on the A8, turn S opposite the harbour on to the B7054 signposted to Largs, then left after passing below the railway on to the B788 signposted Kilmacolm. Follow the B788 as it rises above Greenock, then just before the derestriction sign turn into Leven Road, then Renton Road and next Arden Road. Walk up the hillside behind the houses to the line of pylons; pause at the third pylon from the road, then continue uphill across heather-covered ground beyond a double line of tele-graph poles to the next ridge. If in doubt head for the highest point on the ridge. The electric fence heading uphill hereabouts lies just S of the fortlet-ditch.) The fortlet-ramparts stand 1.6m high, with a single rock-cut ditch now 0.8m deep, interrupted by a causeway to the gate which is placed on the S side. Less certainly there is a second gate in the N rampart. There has been no excavation here, but Roman pottery found on the surface nearby is of Antonine date. A road led S from the fortlet (its course can be detected immediately S of the fortlet across marshy ground) along the line of the Old Largs Road, past Loch Thom. In 1970 a similar fortlet was located on this road at **Outerwards**. (5km S of Loch Thom, turn right on to a farm track to Outerwards farm; follow field boundaries leading uphill behind the farm buildings for about 300m to reach the top of the ridge; then turn right along the spine of the ridge for 300m, till the ground begins to fall away.) The fortlet has a fine prospect over the Firth of Clyde, with the Cowal peninsula, Rothesay and the Cumbrae Islands in view. The near circular ditch survives to a depth of 0.5m, with a low mound preserving some small part of the rampart-stack. There were two small buildings in the interior, located by excavation in 1970. When visited in 1985 the site had been newly traversed by a stone-bottomed estate road, and the rampart damaged by an earthmoving machine. The terminal point of the Roman road could have been Largs, where a fragment of samian pottery was found recently.

It need not be doubted that other forts and fortlets have yet to be located, for example along the upper reaches of the Nith towards the Water of Ayr, and along the Avon river W of Castledykes where a road is known heading due W towards Irvine. A good stretch of this road can be seen at **Dykehead** near Stonehouse. (From the A71 in the W outskirts of Stonehouse take Sidehead Road, signposted Avondyke Training Centre, to a junction, then left on to a minor road marked Kirkmuirhill 4; two field boundaries S of Dykehead farm, which lies just beyond the Training Centre, go left through a grey metal field-gate, and follow the fence downhill to another gate. From there onwards the cambered mound is in view on the left edge of the field.) The embankment stands 0.5m high, and can be followed on foot for 2km to Gil farmhouse (Fig. 22).

Halfway between Castledykes and Irvine Bay was a small fort, of some 3 acres (1.2 ha.) at Loudoun Hill, where a tributary of the River Irvine passes through a defile. The fort is now lost through gravel digging, but excavation between 1938 and 1948 showed several phases of occupation in the Flavian period and renewed occupation at the very beginning of the Antonine period, when it quickly passed out of use. A timber-framed headquarters building and commanding officer's house lay alongside barracks, stables or stores and a granary. Finds (now in the Hunterian Museum) included a bronze hanging lamp and much ironwork, including wagon-wheel tyres, axle fittings and spearheads. The Loudoun Hill fort cannot have stood alone, and a Roman site at the mouth of the River Irvine (which is named *Vindogara* by Ptolemy) has long been postulated. Tacitus tells us that Agricola placed garrisons on the coast facing Ireland: in recent years two marching camps have been found at Girvan, from one of which has come a fragment of 1st-century glass, suggesting that the site belongs in Agricola's time.

D. Redesdale and Tweeddale

For the Romans advancing N from the line of the Tyne at Corbridge the favoured route was by way of the River Rede towards the Tweed at Melrose, and then by the Leader Water towards the Forth at Musselburgh. This route, known from Anglo-Saxon times as Dere Street, is (for the greater part of its length) the line of the modern A68.

There was also a Roman road NE from Corbridge to the river Aln at Learchild, and then to the coast at Berwick where a fort must

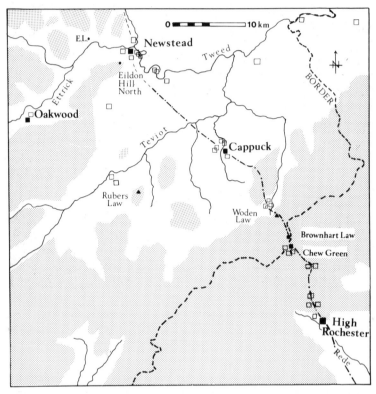

52. **Redesdale, Teviotdale and Tweeddale**. Note: E.L. = Easter Langlee.

surely lie undetected, but no continuation towards Edinburgh (on the line now used by the railway and the A1) is yet known, though isolated finds of Roman material have been plotted along the coasts of Berwickshire and East Lothian.

The course of Dere Street in Northumberland is marked by numerous Roman camps whose defences have survived impressively in upland pastures. Roger Wilson's *Guide to the Roman Remains in Britain* notices the chief sites. Particularly worthy of a visit are forts at Risingham (near the village of West Woodburn) and at High Rochester.

At **Chew Green★★**, N of High Rochester, just before (i.e. on the English side of) the Border, a fortlet and marching camps can be seen in a wild, almost ageless, upland setting which highlights their isolated position. (The visitor on foot may approach from the N via

53. **Chew Green, Northumberland**: aerial view looking N along Dere Street into Scotland. (Photo: Cambridge University Committee for Aerial Photography.)

Pennymuir and Woden Law, starting at Tow Ford; see below for details of this route. Alternatively, direct access to Chew Green may be possible by road from Redesdale army camp at Rochester village; but the visitor using this route must check first that firing is not in progress on adjacent ranges. A whole day is advised for the walk from Chew Green to Pennymuir and back; and possession of the relevant OS 1:50,000 sheet is essential.) Occupation in both Flavian and Antonine periods is likely. The smallest surviving earthwork at Chew Green, but the only one of a permanent nature, is a fortlet of the Antonine period, with a prominent rampart crossed by a causeway to a gate in its NE side, and a triple ditch beyond; there are two small annexes to the E. Nearby is a temporary camp, itself lying within a second camp of 18 acres (7 ha.). The W ditch of the inner camp is particularly impressive, with a depth of 1.5m. Another temporary camp lies to the N. (White marker poles indicate the outer limits of the Roman complex.)

Dere Street now turns to cross a stream (the Chew Sike) and head

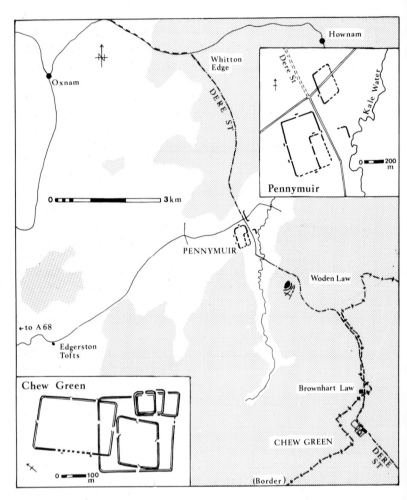

54. Dere Street, from the Border to Whitton Edge; insets: Pennymuir and Chew Green.

N. It survives as a broad flattened mound, sometimes disfigured by mediaeval and more modern trackways. Just 900m N of Chew Green, and almost straddling the Border, is a small fortlet at **Brownhart Law** which observed movement along the Roman road, here closely followed by the Pennine Way; users of the latter, hikers bent against wind and rain, pay the almost invisible Roman site little attention. The low heather-covered rampart of the fortlet, now standing 0.45m high, is enclosed by a double ditch, with a single opening on the E side towards the road. (The site lies close to the fence marking the Border, to the left of the Pennine Way, shortly after the fence, descending from a summit to the left, turns sharply N; beside the Roman road is a large quarry pit.)

The Roman road can now be followed N from Brownhart Law over wild moorland where it survives as a substantial cambered mound, round the N side of Blackhall Hill (the OS 1:50,000 sheet shows a separate pathway running S of this hill) towards **Woden Law**, whose summit is enclosed by the rampart and triple ditches of an Iron Age fort. A little way below them, on the S and E flanks of the hill, are outerworks comprising a triple ditch curving round the hillside, and (further down) a double ditch running N–S which cuts another double ditch. Some have believed these outerworks to represent siegeworks, or practice-works of Roman date; but they may be defensive dykes to be associated with the hillfort itself. The Roman road makes its way round the E side of Woden Law, and descends to cross the Kale Water at **Pennymuir***, where a group of four camps sits to either side of the road. (Car users should leave the A68 at the sign for Edgerston Tofts; after 6km take the minor road signposted Hownam; a further 2km brings the visitor to a T-junction; park there beside a long wooden building. Dere Street underlies the road running S towards the Kale Water at Tow Ford; walk S along Dere Street for 300m to a farm gate on the right.) Lying parallel to the modern road just within a field on the right are the E defences of the largest camp, of 42 acres (17 ha.); just inside the modern gate is one of its gateways, protected by a traverse. Later, a smaller camp was set into the SE corner of the larger, utilising parts of the existing defences. (Now walk forwards at right angles to Dere Street; this line represents the N side of the smaller camp. Continue past a traverse protecting the N gate of the smaller camp, across the interior of the large camp, whose centre is disfigured by a forestry plantation, to its far (W) side, which is reached at another gateway with protecting traverse. The long course of its W rampart (standing 1m high) and the ditch marked by a line of reeds stand out clearly in winter, even better in snow. Turn right and follow the rampart of the large camp to its NW corner and then along the N side, back to the access road.). Two other camps are known at Pennymuir, on the other side of Dere Street: the SW corner of one of these lies just opposite the NE corner of the larger camp just described; the fourth camp lies a little to the S.

Dere Street can be followed N on foot from Pennymuir. (Walk back from Pennymuir camps to the wooden building, then follow a track going directly forward for 5km to **Whitton Edge***, where it survives as a substantial mound flanked by quarry pits; also reached direct from Jedburgh via Oxnam.) Thereafter the road dips to cross the Oxnam Water where a small fort at Cappuck was first investigated in 1886 and further excavated in 1911. There are no meaningful surface traces of the fort today, but the line of Dere Street is visible both N and S of the fort (the road can be followed on foot from Whitton Edge past Cappuck towards Ancrum; but most of the route is unsuitable for cars.) A fragment of a finely sculptured slab bearing the boar-emblem of the Twentieth Legion was recovered from the Cappuck site in 1886; it is now in the Royal Museum of Scotland, Edinburgh.

At Jedburgh 5km to the W of Cappuck are two inscribed Roman altars re-used as building material in the 12th-century Abbey. One is now a lintel stone, at the entrace to the North Stair of the Abbey. (The stone is above your head as you pass through the wooden door leading to the stair; there is a cast in the Abbey Museum.) The other served as a paving slab at the NE corner of the Presbytery; it is now in the Museum. From the information they bear the two altars belong best in the early 3rd century AD and may form evidence of Severan reoccupation at Cappuck, unless some Roman installation in the more immediate vicinity could be envisaged. Built into the S wall of the Undercroft of the Abbey, near its W end, is a squared-off fragment of a third Roman altar, on which some floral motifs can be discerned.

North of Cappuck, the road runs straight for the triple peaks of the Eildon Hills beside the Tweed. At **Newstead**, a village on the E fringe of Melrose, a major complex of Roman sites has been gradually revealed over the years. (From Melrose, take the B6361 for Newstead village; 500m beyond the village where the road stands high above the Tweed and a railway viaduct comes into view, look out for a replica Roman altar on the right-hand verge. This stands close to the fort's NW corner.) Newstead fort, the largest known permanent Roman site in Scotland apart from the legionary bases at Inchtuthil and Carpow, lay immediately above a crossing of the Tweed, in the shadow of the Eildons, which gave the name *Trimontium* (Triple Mountain) to the Roman base. Newstead was excavated between 1905 and 1910, and the resulting report by James Curle, *A Roman Frontier Post and its People* (Glasgow, 1911), has become a classic, and now a book-collectors' item. Little is to be seen on the ground today,

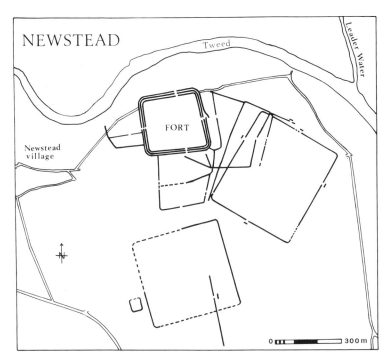

55. **Newstead, Roxburghshire**: fort and nearby marching camps (after RCAHMS).

beyond the flattened-out platform where the fort once stood. The rich assemblage of finds included parade-helmets, metalwork and jewellery, which form an important part of the Roman display in the Royal Museum of Scotland in Edinburgh; a few finds were retained locally and can be seen in the Abbey Museum, Melrose. The fort itself, which faced E (towards the mouth of the Tweed), with its N side protected by a sharp drop to the river, was initially of 10.6 acres (4.3 ha.), though subsequently enlarged to 14.7 acres (6 ha.); it was occupied in both Flavian and Antonine periods, and probably continued in use until about 180 AD, if not later. In the early years of the Antonine occupation the garrison included two cohorts of the Twentieth Legion, together with a regiment of cavalry, the *ala Vocontiorum* originally recruited in southern France; later the site was occupied by a thousand-strong cavalry regiment. The importance of Newstead as a staging post is confirmed by the presence of at least eight camps on the banks of the Tweed between the fort itself and Maxton. One camp,

56. **Bronze face-mask of a cavalryman's helmet**, from Newstead. Highly decorated helmets were worn on special parades. (Photo: National Museums of Scotland.)

lying immediately SE of Newstead fort, is of 165 acres (65 ha.), the southernmost known in a sequence of gigantic enclosures between Tweed and Forth, which seem likely to belong in the Severan age (see Fig. 8).

A Roman inscription recording building activity by the Twenty-Second Legion is set into a garden wall at nearby Abbotsford House, the one-time home of Sir Walter Scott; it may have come originally from Falkirk. (Other sculptured stones walled up in the garden were brought there from a Roman fort at Old Penrith.) At Easter Langlee on the E outskirts of Galashiels a stone building, perhaps a shrine, was found during quarrying in 1965; some marked building-stones were rescued but proper recording of the site was not possible.

The hillfort on **Eildon Hill North** had been a major centre of the Selgovae; nearly 300 circular house-platforms have been plotted in its interior. But such intense occupation did not continue into the Roman period, if we can deduce this from the presence on the summit of a watch-tower, whose single enclosing ditch stands out clearly; within its circle is a cairn of small stones. (The summit can be reached from Melrose by following the sign 'Eildon Walk' on the B6359; but it may be simpler to approach it from the S: at the village of Eildon on the A6091 turn W into a private estate; drive past the house (Eildon Hall) to a pole-barrier; proceed then on foot, forking right at a junction to reach a wooden gate; follow the track uphill – past 'warning' signs for a firing range – to the N peak which is on your right.)

East of Newstead on the lower reaches of the Tweed, aerial reconnaissance has in recent years located several temporary camps, presumably testimony to the progress of a task force heading towards (or penetrating inland from) the mouth of the Tweed at Berwick where a fort must surely have existed.

To the W of Dere Street a number of sites mark Roman penetration into the Southern Uplands along successive river valleys. On the summit of Rubers Law, 3km S of Denholm village, are the defences of a Dark Age stronghold, whose walls incorporated many shaped stones, usually considered Roman. (The hilltop is best reached from Denholmhill farm, off the A698.) The stones (two, with chiselling reminiscent of Roman craftsmanship, are in Hawick Museum) have been seen as evidence for a stone-built watch-tower atop the hill, but such a structure would normally have been of timber, and it could be that we should think rather of a permanent Roman fort or fortlet nearby.

A fort of Flavian date (its ramparts are faintly visible) lay at Oakwood on the Ettrick Water, with a camp nearby. Charred timbers from the structure of the fort gateways were found *in situ* on excavation in 1952; one can be seen (upside down) in Halliwell's House Museum, Selkirk, others are preserved at the Royal Museum of Scotland, Edinburgh.

At Newstead itself a road branched off Dere Street W along the line of the Tweed, more or less on the alignment of the A72 and subsequently the A721. Where the road veered N to follow the Lyne Water, a concentration of permanent posts is to be found at the village of Hallyne (7km W of Peebles), close to the 17th-century Lyne church. Firstly, in the Flavian period, a fort of 3.5 acres (1.4 ha.) was

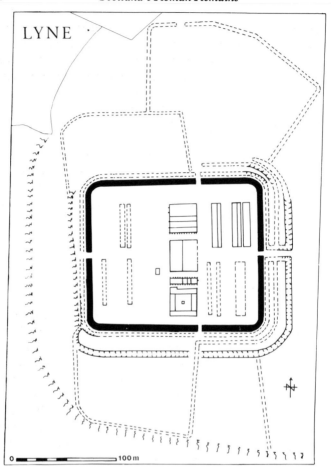

57. **Lyne, Peeblesshire**: ground-plan of the Antonine fort (after RCAHMS).

constructed S of the Lyne Water at Easter Happrew farm, with good views also to both N and S along other river valleys; nothing survives at ground level today. In the Antonine period a different (and in some ways inferior) site was chosen, on the N bank of the Lyne Water where the river made a sharp 90° turn. The ramparts and ditches of the Antonine fort (known today as **Lyne★**), which had an area of 5.6 acres (2.3 ha.), can be followed round much of the perimeter. (Park at Hallyne cottages; walk up the lane leading N to the church, pass through a metal farm-gate and turn sharp left. The plateau on which the fort lies is 200m ahead; you will first enter its E gate across a causeway.) The visible ditch is the outermost of three that originally defended the fort. Turn right to see a fragment of rampart mound at the fort's NE corner, then continue to the NW corner where a similar remnant survives. Continue down the W side of the fort to the SW corner, where a ditch splits off to enclose an annexe stretching to the escarpment above the Lyne Water. Later – but still within the Antonine period – the fort seems to have passed out of use, and a fortlet (not visible) was built just to the N with considerable views to the W along the Lyne Water itself. There are two marching camps lying a little way to the E. West of Lyne the road headed for Castledykes. Along its course were several camps, and a recently identified fortlet at Bankhead near Carnwath.

E. Lauderdale and the Lothians

Northwards from Newstead, the road followed the Leader Water; several camps are known along its route, including one of 165 acres (65 ha.) at Channelkirk, whose once impressive ramparts are now very faint. Nearby at Oxton was a fortlet. Beyond Channelkirk, Dere Street can be followed due N through a forestry plantation to Soutra Aisle. (This stretch is better reached from the N, by turning off the A68 on to the B6368 and parking at woodland just beyond the mediaeval hospice of Soutra Aisle; walk downhill for 100m to reach the cambered mound of the Roman road. The road may be followed downhill, through a gap in the forestry and up the opposite slope.)

Much dressed Roman stonework, including one building block bearing the Pegasus emblem of the Second Legion, was found in 1869 built into a souterrain at Crichton, 6km further to the NW, close to the likely line of Dere Street. This stonework must have derived from a nearby fort, perhaps at Pathhead, but it has not so far been located.

Further N the road went originally (i.e. in the Flavian period) past Eskbank (where there are two camps), to a fort on the North Esk at Elginhaugh beside the A7 trunk road W of Dalkeith, revealed by aerial reconnaissance in 1979. Trial trenching established a Flavian date. Complete excavation of the fort in advance of industrial development took place in 1986. The road presumably continued to the NW (probably on the line of the modern A7), making for Camelon

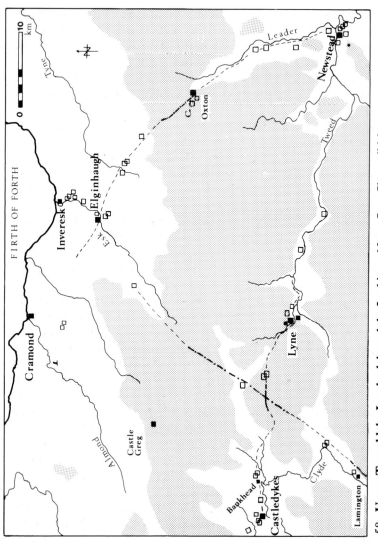

58. **Upper Tweeddale, Lauderdale and the Lothians. Note: C. = Channelkirk.**

fort (below, p. 144). Two marching camps lie more or less on this route. A milestone of Antonine date found at Ingliston and now in the Royal Museum of Scotland shows that the road was refurbished in the Antonine period (Fig. 23). It is clear, however, that during the Antonine period the Elginhaugh site was replaced by a new fort on the Firth of Forth at **Inveresk**, on high ground above a bend in the Esk close to its mouth. Inveresk fort was investigated by Sir Ian Richmond in 1946–47, who established that it faced W and had an area of 6 acres (2.5 ha.); nothing can be seen on the ground, but part of a hypocausted room with a flue leading to a furnace, and four stone pillars supporting a patch of concrete flooring, can be seen in the garden of Inveresk House (ring doorbell for access). This hypocausted room could belong to the fort bath-house, though it lies c. 250m E of the fort itself, and may rather be part of some civilian building. (Note that the placing of the pillars is modern.) Most of the fort is now covered by Inveresk churchyard from which Roman material is recovered from time to time. A substantial civil settlement grew up outside Inveresk, and inscriptions indicate the presence there of an imperial procurator.

Along the S coast of the Forth we may easily suppose a chain of posts protecting the E flank of the Antonine Wall, for example at the mouth of the Water of Leith, and further W at Hopetoun and Blackness. To date, however, only one site on the coast is known, a fort of about 5 acres (2 ha.) at **Cramond*** where the River Almond flows into the Forth. (Take a minor road off the A90 to Cramond at the Barnton Hotel in the W outskirts of Edinburgh; then after nearly 2km, turn left into Cramond Glebe Road. Park opposite the entrance to Cramond Kirk, or further downhill in the car park behind the Cramond Inn. Parts of the fort, excavated in 1954–66, are exposed to view in parkland next to the church.) An information board helps to relate the Roman layout to modern features. Today a pleasant village, with yachts moored by the quayside, Cramond in Roman times can be envisaged as a port of some importance. Occupation in the Flavian period is uncertain, coins forming the only evidence. The visible fort belongs in the Antonine age, and was refurbished at the time of Severus' campaigns. Some occupation, presumably civilian, in later generations down to the 4th century, is attested by the pottery assemblage and coin finds hereabouts. The fort was enclosed by a stone wall, with a clay bank behind. One wall of a stone-built workshop of Severan date has been consolidated for permanent display, and the outlines of parts of two granaries, and between them

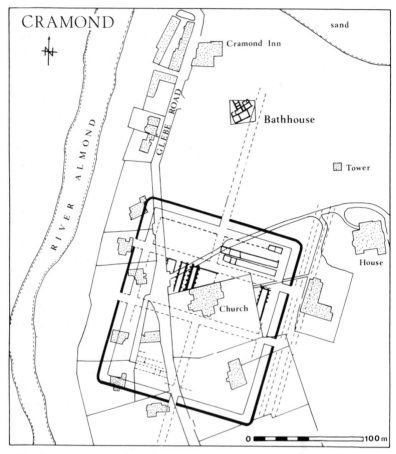

59. **Cramond, West Lothian**: ground-plan of fort and bathhouse (after Holmes; by courtesy of Edinburgh City Museums and Galleries).

the headquarters building, together with a small latrine block in the fort's NE corner, are marked out on the ground. Just beyond the latrine can be seen a length of fort rampart including the NE corner, standing to a height of 0.5m. There is a break in the rampart mound for the E gate. Nearby are the 18th-century Cramond House and the newly restored Cramond Tower.

In 1975, the laying out of the car park behind the Cramond Inn brought to light a large bath-house, its walls standing up to 14 courses in height, which has unfortunately been backfilled through lack of funds to consolidate and display it. The bath-house lies in rough ground beyond the now redundant sign 'Archaeological Excavations: Please Keep Out'! More recently, small-scale work E of the fort has revealed a road leading E, as well as the defensive ditches of the fort and something of a civilian settlement beyond.

On the foreshore 500m W of Cramond, on the far side of the River Almond (reached in a small ferryboat), is a large rock known as **Eagle Rock**. On its E face (i.e. that facing the approaching visitor) is a sculptured figure in a niche, once interpreted as an eagle, but now better seen as Mercury (god of travel and trade) or a Genius (presiding spirit of the locality) holding a cornucopia and sacrificing at a little altar beside his right leg. The sculptural details are hard to make out, and the presence of a protective grille hinders proper appreciation.

It seems likely that Inveresk or Cramond was linked to the Clyde valley by a road running SW along the N flank of the Pentlands. At **Castle Greg***, in the now empty moorland 6km S of West Calder, is a finely preserved fortlet, with rampart and double ditch. (On the B7008 1km N of its junction with the A70, 200m N of a forestry plantation and 150m E of the road.) The site stands against a fine backdrop of the Pentlands, often snowcapped in the winter months. A Flavian date is normally assigned to the site. The fortlet-rampart stands to a height of 1m and the ditches are 2.4m wide and 0.7m deep. There was a single entrance on the E side. Excavation in 1852 recovered Roman pottery from a well in the centre of the fortlet. The road which this fortlet implies could have joined the main Clydesdale–Tweeddale route at or near the newly found Bankhead fortlet (above, p. 109).

CHAPTER 11

The Antonine Wall

The Antonine Wall is Scotland's chief Roman monument. Much of its course of 37 miles (60km) between Forth and Clyde can be followed in a day by car, but several days will be needed by the visitor who wishes to explore its course in detail. But while the visitor to Hadrian's Wall between Tyne and Solway has often merely to look to one side of the modern road to see stonework dramatically positioned on the adjacent crags, the traveller along the Scottish frontier will not find an upstanding barrier confronting him at every point. Like a detective he must follow a trail to identify the traces of rampart-mound and ditch-hollow. These can indeed be followed for over half of the Wall's course; much remains too of the defences of the forts and fortlets placed at intervals along it.

That the Antonine Wall seems less impressive today than its Hadrianic counterpart stems largely from the materials used in its construction. The Antonine Wall was a *rampart* of laid turf, set on a stone foundation some 15 Roman feet (4.3m) wide, with neatly dressed kerbs enclosing a rubble core. The turf superstructure, which must have attained a height of about 3.6m, today survives to a maximum height of about 1.6m; for the most part the visitor will see no more than a low mound, and at times only a skin of turfwork may survive on top of the stone base. (A stretch of 15km of the Wall, at the E end of the Forth–Clyde line, was in fact built not of turf but of earth held in place by narrow turf cheeks.) Precisely how the rampart-stack was 'finished off' on top is not known; probably there was a rampart-walk, with wooden duckboards.

It is the *ditch* which has survived as the more recognisable feature today. Sometimes it can be seen merely as a shallow dip in the ground along a field boundary or across a hillside; at other times, however, it presents the visitor with a formidable barrier, preserving almost its original dimensions of up to 40 feet (12m) in breadth and 12 feet (3.6m) in depth. It was not intended as a moat, but must on occasion, then as now, have been partly filled with water through natural

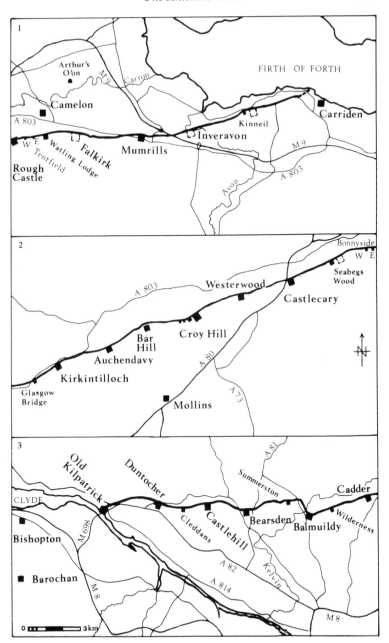

60. **The Antonine wall**: general map showing forts, mile-fortlets and expansions along its line, from E to W.

61. Stone rampart-base of the Antonine Wall at Hillfoot Cemetery, Bearsden, looking E. (Photo: L. Keppie.)

62. Ditch of the Antonine Wall at Watling Lodge, Falkirk, looking E. (Photo: L. Keppie.)

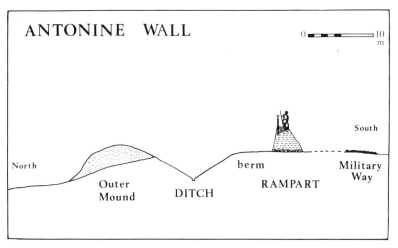

63. Antonine Wall: cross-section through the defences.

drainage. Large stones, set at regular intervals, marked the edges of the ditch; the spoil was thrown out on the N side where it formed a substantial mound. Just behind the Wall ran a road, some 6m wide, of rough cobbles topped by gravel. This road, known today as the *Military Way*, provided a lateral communications link for the garrisons of the various forts.

Along the Wall at intervals of about 2 miles (3.5km) were *forts*, most but not all attached to the rear of the Wall itself, which formed their N ramparts. The sites of 15 forts are securely known, and 4 more are suspected on grounds of spacing. However, it seems that when the Romans arrived on the Forth–Clyde isthmus and began the construction of the barrier, they planned to have only 6 forts, widely spaced at about 8-mile (14km) intervals. The gaps between them were filled by *fortlets*, attached to the Wall at roughly one-mile intervals; 9 of these 'mile-fortlets' are known, and at least 30 more may await discovery. However, while the Wall was still under construction, there was a change of plan, and many more forts were added to the frontier line, to bring the total up to the 19 we know of or suspect today. Why the additional forts were built we cannot precisely say, except that a much closer surveillance of the frontier line must have been thought necessary. There are also six *expansions*, set against the back of the rampart, which may have served as signalling platforms; and near Wilderness Plantation (below, p. 134) are three *ditched enclosures* recently detected at the back of the Wall, but their purpose is not yet clear. In the immediate vicinity of the Wall were numerous *camps* (not shown on Fig. 60) which must have housed work-squads engaged on the construction of the barrier and of the forts and fortlets, but no traces of them are visible at ground level.

The precise starting point of the Wall itself on the River Forth has not so far been determined, but it seems clear that the E terminus of the frontier was protected by a fort of some 4 acres (1.6 ha.) at Carriden on the E outskirts of Bo'ness, directly overlooking the Forth. (Turn off the A904 at Muirhouses, going E on to a minor road into Carriden Estate.) The fort was found from the air in 1945, when the triple ditches forming its E defences were noted in farmland E of Carriden House; the greater part of the fort lies within the wooded grounds of the House. In 1956 an altar to Jupiter dedicated by the residents of a village (*vicus*) beside the fort was ploughed up here, useful testimony to the existence of a civil settlement. The Latin inscription also gives the Roman name for the fort: *Velunia* (or *Veluniate*). Aerial photography has revealed substantial traces of cultivation- and drainage-ditches nearby.

In 1868 a large commemorative tablet or 'distance slab' was turned up on the SE slope of Bridgeness promontory, near the 18th-century Bridgeness Tower (built originally as a windmill), some 1.2km W of Carriden fort; it has been generally assumed that the Wall began thereabouts, but a recent excavation close by the findspot of the slab failed to detect any traces of Wall or ditch. It remains possible that the Wall started further E, perhaps near Carriden itself. A modern slab inscribed with a copy of the Latin text was placed to mark the findspot of the distance slab (on the W side of Harbour Road, near the Tower), but it has suffered badly from the weather, and the Latin wording is now almost illegible.

On the high ground above Bridgeness promontory, it can be assumed that the Wall underlies Grahamsdyke Road and its westwards continuation, Dean Road (the present-day A993), after which it enters the grounds of Kinneil House, a 16th-century mansion with fine wall and ceiling frescoes. A fort as yet unlocated could be looked for at Kinneil House. Beyond the House in an area formerly covered by a mediaeval village (of which only the ruined 12th-century church now remains), the Antonine ditch can be discerned as a hollow running W in rolling farmland, now designated a Leisure Area. The Military Way too can be seen as a slight ridge running parallel to the

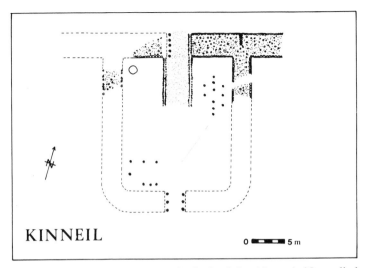

KINNEIL

0 ▮▭▮▭▮ 5 m

64. **Kinneil**: ground-plan of the mile-fortlet (after Murray). Note: ditches not shown.

ditch about 50m behind it. (Park at Kinneil House, cross the stream behind the House, and the Chapel soon comes into view on the right. The single tree in the field beyond sits on the N edge of the ditch.)

Beyond a small reservoir the ditch can be picked up again; here on a little hilltop are displayed the remains of a mile-fortlet, originally located by trial trenching in 1978, and completely exposed for public display in 1981. The fortlet (named **Kinneil★**) measures some 18m E–W by some 21m N–S, and was defended by a rampart of earth revetted by turf cheeks, set on a stone base, and by one or perhaps two ditches. There were gates in the N and S sides, with timber-framed towers above. The outlines of the rampart are marked on the ground by concrete slabs. The positions and layouts of the gateways and of two small buildings in the interior of the fortlet are marked by modern timbers placed in the original post-holes. A cobbled road flanked by drains ran through the fortlet from N to S. Finds from the fortlet are displayed in Kinneil Museum (near the House).

West of Kinneil the Wall follows high ground more or less on the 60m (200 feet) contour line and overlooking the Grangemouth petro-chemical complex, before descending the slope beside Inveravon Tower, a remnant of the 15th-century Inveravon Castle, towards the river Avon itself. Close to the river, excavation in 1967 located walling and streets, and fieldwalking close to the river's edge has produced flue-tiles and bricks suggestive of a bath-house. Such a bath-house could belong with a fort which on grounds of spacing would be suspected nearby, either on the low ground beside the Avon (but aerial reconnaissance over many years has failed to detect any un-equivocal traces) or on high ground beside Inveravon Tower.

On the W bank of the Avon the ditch is clearly seen running up the slope towards the golf-clubhouse of **Polmonthill**, but the line of the rampart itself is now obscured by an artificial ski-slope, which threatens to engulf this whole stretch. Further W, on the far side of the golf course, a fine stretch of ditch, seldom visited today, can be seen in **Millhall Wood** behind an 'equestrian course'. (Best reached from the B904 by turning into a car park opposite Little Kerse Riding School; follow a path uphill straight ahead, then after 50m veer to the left to reach the crest of the slope; the hollow of the ditch should now be in view.) The Wall next rises towards Polmont Village, where the 19th-century church with its twin spires, all but overlying the frontier line, provides a useful landmark. A long stretch of the frontier line was destroyed with the building of the M9 motorway in the 1960s. After crossing low ground at Beancross, the Wall now approaches the farm at Mumrills, where there stood the largest fort on the Wall line, some 6.5 acres (2.6 ha.) in size, excavated in 1923–28 and in 1958–60. The outlines of the fort (roughly bounded by Beancross Road, Sandy Loan and the A803 to Falkirk) are detectable from the air. Two regiments are known to have served at Mumrills: the *Ala Tungrorum*, a cavalry unit from the Lower Rhineland, and the Second Cohort of Thracians, from Bulgaria.

West of Mumrills the course of the Wall is concealed below housing in the old village of Laurieston, before crossing the A803 to enter the grounds of the **Forth Valley College of Nursing** (formerly Callendar Park College of Education) where the ditch is well preserved, and then into the parkland which once formed the grounds of **Callendar House***. (Turn left off the A903 into Callendar Park, then left into Seaton Place; park at the end of the road beside Symon Tower, and walk N until the ditch-hollow comes into view.) Here the ditch is still a formidable obstacle, some 60 feet (18m) across, and the accompany-ing rampart survives as a low mound.

West of Callendar Park the Wall is lost below high-rise flats before descending to the course of the now canalised East Burn. At **Kemper Avenue** beside the Burn a routine investigation in 1980, in search of the Wall before the construction of a car park, revealed an oblong building equipped with underfloor central heating, possibly a bath-house. The car park was subsequently shortened to leave the site of the Roman building undamaged, and the course of the rampart has been indicated by careful landscaping; some of the dressed kerb-stones are visible, and an 'ancient monument' board has been erected. (Reached from the A903 by turning left at a roundabout into Arnot Street, then into Kemper Avenue; the stone base lies at the far end of the car park on the left.)

Thereafter the Wall climbed to high ground S of Falkirk town centre, where a fort has long been presumed in the area known as the Pleasance. To the W of the town-centre the visitor can pick up the Ditch again at **Bantaskin** where a length of 200m survives amid a housing development. (W of the town centre, turn S off the A903 beside a whisky distillery into Glenfuir Road, then into Anson Avenue; follow the road to the top of the ridge and park in a small, half-concealed layby on the left; the ditch lies in wooded ground above.) Continuing W, the visitor should now follow Glenfuir Road (the B816) to the Barr soft-drink factory, then right into Tamfourhill Road. Almost immediately beyond on the left there begins a fine stretch of ditch, with the low mound of the rampart visible on its S side, at **Watling Lodge**★★. Here the N face of the ditch had been substantially made up in antiquity to increase the efficacy of the obstacle which is still 12m across and 5m deep. Just behind the villa of Watling Lodge (part of which stands silhouetted in the ditch at the W end of the visible stretch) was a mile-fortlet excavated in 1972–74 prior to housing development. A road led N from the fortlet to the fort at Camelon.

Beyond Watling Lodge the ditch crosses low and rather marshy ground to reach again the B816, after which it enters **Tentfield Plantation**★, where it can be followed without serious interruption for 2km as far as Rough Castle. The remains of both ditch and rampart are particularly impressive here, in the peaceful wooded setting of the plantation, especially in winter when the trees have shed their leaves and the bracken in the ditch is depressed. Soon after entering the woodland, the ditch is crossed by a metal footbridge, in the garden of a house called Tayavalla ('the house on the Wall'). A signal-platform or 'expansion' (known as **Tentfield East**) can be seen here as a mound some 10m square attached to the rear of the rampart (opposite the entrance to Rowan Crescent). Something can be seen of the original turf layering of the rampart, when it is exposed by motorcycle enthusiasts who have favoured the Wall hereabouts as an adventure course. The walker can now continue W, either following the rampart-mound, or crossing to the N side of the ditch, until the line of the frontier is cut by a quarry access road. Just before the Wall descends to cross the quarry road, there is another 'expansion' (**Tentfield West**), attached to the S side of the rampart-mound, but it is not easy to see in the under-growth. To either side of the quarry road the cambered mound of the Military Way is visible to the S of the Wall, beyond the double line of electricity poles. Continue along the line of the ditch, which is much disfigured by pit-heaps. Another turn to the W leads to a long straight stretch of rampart-mound and ditch; next, a stile heralds arrival at the Guardianship area of Rough Castle. (For the car user, it is advisable to turn back at the quarry road, drive to Rough Castle along the B816 via High Bonnybridge; AM signs for Rough Castle. Turn right on to a minor road (new access) 100m S of the Smith & Wellstood factory, whose end-wall is decorated with an award-winning but now rather faded mural showing former industrial activities within. Continue along the minor road, across the railway, past

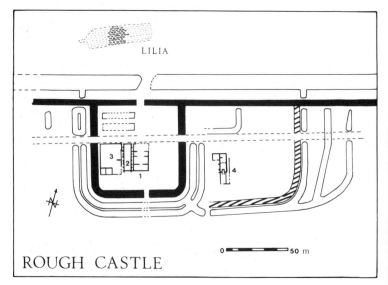

65. **Rough Castle on the Antonine Wall**: ground-plan of the fort (after MacIvor, Thomas and Breeze). Note: 1 = headquarters, 2 = granary, 3 = commanding officer's house, 4 = bathhouse.

Bonnyside House, after which rampart and ditch, preserved in rough ground on the left, come into view, to a cattle grid marking the entrance to the Guardianship area; there is car parking, and the fort lies on the plateau beyond the Rowan Tree Burn.)

The fort at **Rough Castle**** is probably the most visited military installation on the Antonine Wall: its rampart stands to a height of 1m, and the plan of the defensive ditches is clear. The fort was small, scarcely more than one acre (0.4 ha.). There were four gates, one in each side, with causeways crossing the ditches to reach them. The visitor should begin outside the N gate, and enter the fort by the causeway across the broad Antonine ditch. Straight ahead were the headquarters building and (to its right) a granary and the command-

66. **Rough Castle on the Antonine Wall**: aerial view from the W. Note the course of the ditch running from bottom to top in the photograph, and the *lilia* (left foreground). (Photo: RCAHMS.)

ing officer's house, excavated in 1902–3, and left exposed to public gaze. Turning right to the W gate of the fort, the visitor can look down over the course of the Rowan Tree Burn. On the slope are two ditches cut by a causeway. Next follow the rampart round to the S gate, and go on to the E gate, which gave access into an annexe. Just to the right (inside the annexe) was the fort bath-house. On the left (also within the annexe) is a shallow ditch turning at right angles, which may have enclosed a mile-fortlet, later replaced by the visible fort. The annexe is defended on the E by three separate ramparts and ditches, which may testify to successive reductions in its size. Part of the Sixth Cohort of Nervians, originally raised from a Belgic tribe which offered stout resistance to Caesar, formed the garrison for a time, under the command of a legionary centurion.

Returning to the N gate, the visitor should cross the Antonine ditch by the broad causeway and walk a little to the NW till a group of oblong pits comes into view. These are the remnants of a substantial system comprising ten rows of about 20 pits, set diagonally; the pits, once 0.9m deep, probably held upright sharpened stakes, concealed from general view by brushwood. They must have been a considerable obstacle to the unsuspecting attacker, who would fall into them without warning, to be impaled on the stakes. Pits of this type are described by Caesar – whose soldiers called them *lilia* ('lilies'), from a resemblance to that flower with its vertical stem and enclosing leaves. The 'lilies' at Rough Castle can still claim victims among the unwary today.

West of Rough Castle fort, the profile of the Antonine ditch and rampart stands clear against the skyline, across the Rowan Tree Burn. The rampart survives here to a height of 1.6m or more, the highest anywhere along the Wall. Another 'expansion' (**Bonnyside East**) can just be made out, attached to S side of the rampart, some 50m west of the entrance to the Guardianship area. It was excavated in 1957 and proved to measure about 5.3m square, constructed of turf on a stone base. A further 'expansion' (**Bonnyside West**), this time better preserved, lies within the private grounds of Bonnyside House, just beyond the stone dyke, at a point where the Wall and ditch make a turn to the SW towards the modern village of Bonnybridge. The ditch-hollow, often filled with water or reeds, can easily be followed into the distance. It was near this spot that the legendary Scottish chieftain, Graham, broke through the Antonine Wall which in local traditions was for long to bear his name as Grahamsdyke. In truth, however, the name 'Grahamsdyke' (which survives today as a street-name at several points along the Wall) is 'grymisdyke', i.e. the strong wall. Graham and his exploits have no foundation in history.

For a while the Wall is lost in modern Bonnybridge, before emerging in front of Seabegs Place farmhouse (just S of the B816), beyond which a fine stretch of the frontier can be seen in **Seabegs Wood**★: ditch, upcast, rampart mound and (some 50m to the S) the Military Way are all present; excavation of the Military Way in 1962 showed that the road was c. 7m wide. On a little plateau just beyond the W edge of the wood, on the lands of Dalnair, excavation in 1977 revealed the outlines of a mile-fortlet. A fort could be expected hereabouts on grounds of spacing, but attempts to locate it have proved unsuccessful.

The Wall now continues W towards the village of Allandale. A short length of ditch survives N of the B816 just E of a newly laid out car park. In Allandale itself the ditch can just be seen as a hollow on the N side of the road, W of a bowling green. Before the junction of the B816 with the A80 trunk road, the outline of the ditch-hollow is visible against the E boundary wall of the former Castlecary Primary School (now a nine-apartment villa). A fort, of 3.5 acres (1.4 ha.) with an annexe to the E, occupied the plateau at **Castlecary** overlooking the Red Burn, with a fine view N through the Denny Gap. (Turn left off the B816 just after the School, then left again to a cottage. The fort lies in the field opposite the front of the School; there is an information board.) Castlecary fort is mentioned by antiquarians from the mid-17th century onwards, and was comprehensively dug in 1902; the fort was defended by a wall of stone, and the central buildings were stone-built. Little was learned about barracks or stores. Inscriptions found here over the years testify to the presence of a First Cohort of Vardullians (from N Spain) and a First Cohort of Tungrians (from Belgium), as well as groups of legionaries. The site had already been much disturbed in 1841 by the building of the Edinburgh to Glasgow railway line which bisects the site. Today little can be seen, though some stonework of the fort-wall on the E side can be made out in the field where there is a distinct ridge, and a clump of trees marks the location of the headquarters building and a granary, left exposed in 1902. A short length of the fort's N wall can be seen in a depression against the N boundary wall of the field. Stonework from Castlecary fort was transported to the nearby Castle Cary, a 15th-century tower-house; in the garden wall of the Castle is one building stone ornamented with a horizontal phallic symbol.

West of Castlecary, the Wall descends to the Red Burn, then climbs to high ground occupied by Avonside Homes factory, a new landmark for travellers. (Continue on the B816 across the A80.) At **Garnhall** beyond the railway, the ditch becomes visible again, and rapidly becomes very impressive. (Reached from a minor road beside the Castlecary Hotel, by way of worn stone steps in the side of a field dyke; AM signpost.) Passing in front of the now-demolished farmstead of Garnhall (where some of the edging stones of the ditch may be discerned through the grass), it continues (beyond a minor road) into the former lands of **Tollpark** where it runs just N of industrial premises and later a grassy airstrip. Some 350m W of the minor road, a short stretch of stone base, exposed by water action over the centuries, can be made out; it is c. 4.5m wide and incorporates a culvert. The ditch continues as a formidable barrier, with the upcast mound topped by a line of trees, a useful guide at a distance to its alignment. Beyond Tollpark, the Wall descends to the site of **Westerwood** fort, where the farm buildings which lie within the fort's NE quarter have been refurbished to house a Jubilee Youth Centre. (The fort can also be approached direct from a minor road leading N from the B816 at a roundabout opposite the Old Inns service station.) Westerwood fort, excavated in 1932, was small, scarcely more than 2 acres (0.8 ha.). The rampart, a double ditch (visible now as a single hollow), and upcast beyond are visible along the S flank of the fort, and especially at its SE corner. Farm outbuildings constructed on top of the E defences are held together against subsidence by iron clamps. An altar to Silvanus, god of the woodland, was found W of the fort in 1963 (now at Kinneil Museum; above, p. 119); excavation to the S in 1974–75 failed to detect traces of civil settlement. On high ground at Carrickstone, 1.5km to the S and best reached from Cumbernauld village, there stands a Roman altar, close to a concrete water-tower. It is the only altar in Scotland still exposed to the elements. No part of an inscription is now visible, and how the altar came to be at Carrickstone remains unknown. Beyond Westerwood, the Wall continued through open country towards Dullatur. Just E of **East Dullatur House*** (by car best reached from Dullatur village; AM sign), a fine stretch of ditch can be seen, some 12m across and 3.5m deep.

West of the Dullatur–Kilsyth road on the lands of Wester Dullatur farm the ditch shows merely as a dip along the modern field boundary, but the dip gradually broadens and deepens until it reaches **Croy Hill**** where, beyond an embankment which once supported a

67. **Sculptured relief showing three legionaries,** from Croy Hill on the Antonine wall. (Photo: National Museums of Scotland.)

mineral railway, it assumes its full dimensions and can be followed uphill to Croy fort. (Best approached along a farm track off the Dullatur–Kilsyth Road about halfway between Wester Dullatur farm and the canal bridge at Craigmarloch.) The particular reason for the splendid state of preservation hereabouts is that the ditch was cut out of solid rock – the hard basalt of which the hill itself is largely composed. The spoil from the ditch, thrown out on the N side to form an upcast mound, remains almost as the Romans left it, its rocky make-up having resisted centuries of land improvement; meanwhile, the rampart (of turf on a stone base) has left few visible traces. We can easily imagine the consternation of the Roman work-squad detailed to dig the ditch over Croy Hill on finding rock beneath their feet instead of the usual clay or sand! No description is required for the visitor climbing the slope towards the summit. There on the E shoulder of the Hill is the site of a fort, the position of which is indicated by a small group of trees. The low stone-built walls visible hereabouts are not remnants of Roman buildings but of an 18th-century farmhouse. Limited trenching on the fort-site in 1920, 1931 and 1935 established its outlines (about 1.5 acres/0.6 ha. overall) and located some internal buildings. Several inscribed stones indicate the presence of a detachment from the Sixth legion *Victrix*. In 1975–78 areas W, S and E of the fort were investigated in advance of the quarrying which threatens to alter the land contours hereabouts beyond recognition in the next few years. Some evidence of cultivation and human habitation was found, together with spectacular small finds including a bronze arm-purse (see Fig. 27) and part of a terracotta face-mask. Some 25m E of the fort a short stretch of the ditch remained undug, perhaps the result of a changeover in work-squads hereabouts.

To the W of the fort the ditch can be followed as an irregular cut on the N flank of Croy Hill which is so steep hereabouts that formal defence seems hardly necessary. Some 75m W of Croy fort was a mile-fortlet, sited on a flat-topped hillock, first noted and tested by excavation in 1977–78. Further W as the ground drops away and **Croy Village★** comes into view, two 'expansions' can be seen, attached to the rear of the Wall some 140m apart. They survive impressively to a height of c. 1.5m.

The ditch can be followed down to the village, where it is lost beside a rather unattractive quarry and lorry park. Thereafter it crosses low ground, N of the Olde Duke public house, and continues W across the modern B802 in line with a track which leads W off that road towards Bar Hill (AM signpost). Nothing can be seen until the track peters out in open ground recently landscaped. A clear strip in the forestry plantation marks the line of the Military Way heading uphill towards Bar Hill. The visitor should turn right to reach higher ground where the ditch will become visible. From this point the visitor on foot enjoys a long vista, as the ditch stretches into the distance, a cleared strip in the plantation, much as it may have looked in Roman times. After several sharp descents the ditch rises to skirt the north flank of **Castle Hill** where it overlies part of the outer defences of a small Iron Age hillfort. At one point on the hillside the ditch seems not to have been fully dug out, perhaps because of the rock beneath. A climb to the top of Castle Hill, the summit topped by a triangulation pillar, is well worthwhile, for it provides a view not only back to Croy, Westerwood and Castlecary, but also W to the now adjacent Bar Hill fort, and beyond it along the south flank of the Kelvin valley to

Bearsden and even beyond. The watery stripe of the Forth & Clyde Canal follows the Wall's alignment westwards into the distance, with the slopes of the Campsie Hills rising on the N side of the valley. The Roman fort of Castlehill (Bearsden) – not to be confused with the locality currently being described – with *its* summit crowned by a distinctive circle of beech trees, is in view on a clear day, fully 18Km to the W, forming a convenient guide to the alignment of the frontier. Descending from Castle Hill by a winding path, the visitor arrives directly at the E gate of Bar Hill fort, while the Antonine Ditch has veered away to the right before passing along the N side of the fort towards Twechar village.

Bar Hill* fort, which the visitor now approaches, is among the best-known fort-sites on the line of the Antonine Wall. First noticed by antiquarians in the 17th century, it was comprehensively excavated in 1902–1905. The fort covered an area of about 3.2 acres (1.3 ha.), with a rampart of turf on a stone base, defended by two ditches except on the N side where there was a single ditch. The fort was not set directly, like all but one of those we have met with, against the Wall itself – the latter passed by about halfway down the N flank of Bar Hill while the fort sits squarely on its summit. The visitor entering by the E gate crosses the double ditch on a causeway which marks the line of the Military Way and should walk directly forward to the true summit of the Hill. Here facing on to the *via principalis* is the stone headquarters building, laid out for public view after re-excavation in 1979–82. There is an information board from which the main features and structures can be conveniently viewed. (By car it is simplest to reach Bar Hill from the W, via the B8023, turning S into Twechar village; AM signpost. Park at or opposite the war memorial in Twechar village, and walk uphill past the now renovated Bar farm to the top of the hill. Shortly before the saucer-shaped water tank, turn left along a field boundary to reach the fort-site with its now scanty covering of trees. In this case the visitor will arrive at the fort's SW corner; he should go directly to the summit of the Hill, to the information board.)

The plan of the headquarters building is easily comprehended: the largest compartment was the front courtyard, with a stone-lined well in its E half. Behind was a covered assembly hall, and at the back a set of three rooms, of which the central compartment constituted the regimental chapel. From the 13m-deep well came numerous stone column shafts and capitals, the wooden well-bucket, pulley wheel and

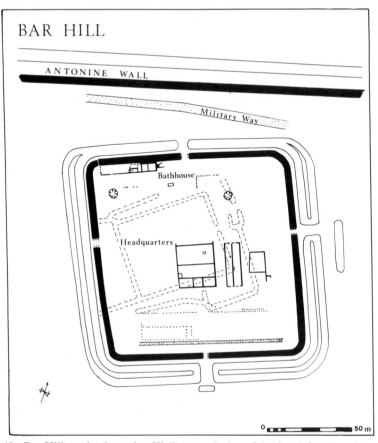

BAR HILL

ANTONINE WALL

Military Way

Bathhouse

Headquarters

0   50 m

68. Bar Hill on the Antonine Wall: ground-plan of the fort (after Keppie). Dotted lines represent the outlines of an underlying 'ditched enclosure' of uncertain date and function.

winding gear, ironwork and coins (now on display in the Hunterian Museum). The S rampart of the fort followed the line of the modern field boundary. More can be seen of the W rampart and ditches, and the visitor should proceed along the *via principalis* to the W gateway, marked by a gap in the rampart. Turning then to the right, he can follow the rampart (and accompanying ditch-hollow) N to the NW corner of the fort, just inside which lay a small bath-house (information board). At its W end were latrines, and further E was a small hypocausted room heated by a little furnace. This was the 'hot dry' room.

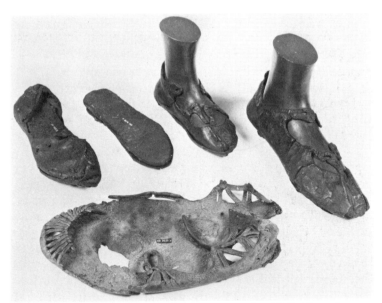

69. **Leather shoes**, from Bar Hill on the Antonine Wall. Shoes for men, women and children can be distinguished. (Photo: Hunterian Museum.)

70. **Wooden wagon-wheel**, made of ash with a one-piece iron tyre; from Bar Hill. (Photo: Hunterian Museum.)

Further E were three heated rooms, and beyond them was a furnace; one of the capstones from its main flue has been placed to indicate its original position. Walking E from the bath-house, the visitor quickly reaches the site of the N gate (faintly visible as a dip in the rampart mound), with a causeway across the single N ditch. At the fort's NE corner, a stone-lined culvert carried water through the rampart from the fort on the hilltop above. Inscriptions show that Bar Hill was garrisoned by the First Cohort of Hamians, a specialist archer unit from Syria, and later by the First Cohort of Baetasians from the Rhineland. A broken altar, perhaps from Bar Hill, recording Tanicius Verus, commanding officer of a regiment of auxiliaries, is now in Colzium House Museum, Kilsyth.

Leaving Bar Hill by the modern gate at the SW corner of the fort, the visitor descends by the farm track to Bar farm, near which the Antonine Ditch, having passed by the fort, draws near again, and its hollow is easily made out on the right of the track. Beyond Twechar village, the Wall swings to the left past the farmhouse of Shirva (where several graveslabs and other commemorative stones were dug up from the wreckage of what may have been a souterrain in 1728–29). Gradually the faint depression of the ditch can again be made out N of the B8023 as it approaches the farmhouse and steading of **Auchendavy**, which lie within the defences of a fort of some 2.7 acres (1.1 ha.); no excavation has taken place but the outlines are still visible on the ground, especially on the E side where there is a distinct ditch-hollow, and on the N front, where a possible causeway is faintly visible across the Antonine Ditch. The modern road runs through the fort on the line of its *via principalis*. Aerial photographs show that the fort was defended by three ditches. Numerous sculptured stones, built into the farmhouse and its adjuncts, were noted by the antiquarians, but all have disappeared from view. Five altars, found in a pit S of the fort in 1771 while the Canal was being dug, were erected by Marcus Cocceius Firmus, a legionary centurion, perhaps a one-time commanding officer at the fort. These altars, and the sculptures from Shirva, are in the Hunterian Museum.

West of Auchendavy fort, the ditch is soon lost below the embankment of the Canal. The visitor would do well now to go straight to Kirkintilloch (via the High Street, Cowgate and Union Street), to Peel Park in the centre of the town, which marks the site of the next fort on the Wall. Its precise outlines are not known, but limited excavation in the park in the 1950s established the alignment of the Wall (a small but disappointing stretch of stone base, with the sad remnants of a

culvert, is on view behind high railings at the NW corner of the Park),
and confirmed that the fort lay on the rearward slope of the hill, with a
splendid view across the Kelvin to the Campsie Hills. The older
antiquarians assumed without question that the mediaeval Peel tower
(a motte now laid out as a feature within the park at its NE corner) was
the Roman fort of old; in fact the Peel straddles the Roman Wall and
part of the fort.

West of the fort-site the Wall disappears again in modern Kirkintilloch, until it emerges into open farmland at Adamslie. However, little
can be made out before Glasgow Bridge, where the modern A803,
recently realigned, crosses the Canal. Just E of the bridge, on higher
ground above some cottages, was a mile-fortlet, seen from the air in
1951. The Wall turns slightly N to pass below the modern road, and
soon the hollow of the ditch can be made out on the right as the
modern road reaches the Hungryside roundabout. (Here the motorist
should turn left on the A803, and may return to the line of the Wall
1km further on via a minor road on the right signposted to Cawder
Church.)

The Wall continues W from the roundabout in a straight line just
clear of factory premises till it reaches the site of Cadder fort where
the Forth & Clyde Canal, which has again come close up against the
Wall, turns sharply to the S just beyond the line of the fort's defences.
The fort itself was entirely lost through gravel extraction in the 1930s
and 1940s. However, excavation in 1929–31 established the outlines,
and revealed the layout of the internal buildings. Beyond the Canal
the Wall passes into the private grounds of Cawder Golf club,
formerly Cawder House, the family home of the Stirlings of Keir.
Built into a locker room of the House is a stone commemorative tablet,
recording building work by men of the Second Legion *Augusta*.
Vestiges of the ditch are hard to detect across the golf course before
the Wall emerges on to higher ground at Wilderness Plantation. (To
reach this point the motorist needs to retrace his steps from Cawder
Church to the A803, then follow it towards Glasgow for 1.5km before
turning right at Eagle Lodge. About 1km after a Sports Centre, the
road turns sharply left; here it rejoins the line of the Wall.) A long
stretch of the Wall's course running W from this point was lost by
quarrying, though the ground has since been restored. Just N of a zig-
zag in the modern road a mile-fortlet was revealed from the air in 1951
at Wilderness Plantation, and excavated in advance of expected
quarrying in 1965–66. (The quarrying never took place.) The ditch

can be followed W from this point, as a hollow in open farmland N of
the road, and where it is crossed by the modern road a short deeper
stretch is filled with water, a good indicator of its position. Just E of
this point aerial reconnaissance has revealed three so-called 'ditched
enclosures' attached to the rampart; one (at Buchley farm) was
excavated in 1980, without clarifying its function. From Wilderness
Plantation to the Centurion Brickworks, the modern road overlies the
Roman ditch, before the latter veers away N opposite a 'City of
Glasgow' boundary sign to descend to the site of Balmuildy fort on a
low plateau overlooking the River Kelvin, with fine views up the
valley of the Blane Water. Balmuildy was excavated in 1912–14 and
much of its layout established, including a stone headquarters building, commanding officer's house and granaries set within a stone
rampart-wall, as well as two bath-houses, one inside the fort, and the
other (more elaborate) within an annexe E of the fort. The fort itself,
with an area of 4 acres (1.6 ha.), was built before the Wall itself, with
projecting 'wing-walls' designed to join up with the Wall when its
builders reached Balmuildy. Nothing can be made out on the ground
today, though re-excavation, as part of a visitor-centre project,
is proposed.

Next the Wall turns sharply N to cross the Kelvin. Large dressed
sandstone blocks, parts of the piers of a bridge crossing the river here,
were dredged up in 1941 and in 1982; the blocks were conspicuous by
the cramp-holes recessed into their sides to hold them fast together
against the surge of the river. Two still lie on the N embankment.

Beyond the river the Wall heads due N (beside the A879) to the
heights of Summerston, where the ditch can be observed turning
sharply to the W behind some cottages. After crossing the A879 it
ascends to the summit of Crow Hill; on the E slope of the hill a mile-
fortlet was identified in 1980. Westwards from the summit of the Hill
the ditch-line can be followed along field boundaries until it crosses
the B8049. On the W side of the road embankment here, the hollow of
the ditch is visible as it crosses a small field before entering Douglas
Park Golf Course. Following the natural crest of the ground it next
reaches **Hillfoot Cemetery★**. Here two fine stretches of the stone base
can be seen, exposed during lanscaping in the cemetery in 1922. The
visitor entering the cemetery should veer to the right to reach its E
boundary-wall on the crest of the hill, where close to and all but
protruding from the modern ground surface is the stone base of the
Antonine Wall, 4.3m wide with finely dressed kerbs and rubble core
incorporating a drainage culvert. (AM information plaque.) The

second stretch of visible base lies further down the hillside, nearer the cemetery entrance. Because the Wall has turned sharply S following ground contours, the second stretch appears to visitors (and indeed is) at right angles to the first, the cause of some confusion! The base here, where it descends a sharp slope, was built originally to the standard width of 4.3m, but was subsequently broadened to 5m, and a second layer of stones was laid down on the upper part of the slope, perhaps to improve stability of the overlying turfwork after a collapse. This stretch too incorporates a culvert.

Soon after, the Wall turns again to the W (a faint curving hollow in the cemetery marks the line of the ditch), and can be followed across the boundary fence into rough ground beyond. Here both ditch and rampart-mound can be observed along the N ends of gardens of **Boclair Road**, except where shielded from view by impenetrable hedges, until they are finally lost among trees and shrubbery. Returning to the cemetery, the visitor should now proceed by way of Boclair Road, across the road junction with the A81 at the bottom of the hill, into Roman Road, so named because it follows the line of the Military Way. The Wall itself ran along the S lip of a defile containing the Manse Burn.

Soon the modern road rises to a plateau which marked the site of the next fort, **Bearsden★**, passing through the site on the line of the fort's *via principalis*; the fort thus lies both N and S of the modern road. Over the last decade the entire N half of the fort and its annexe has been redeveloped, with four large sandstone mansions of the Victorian age replaced by numerous maisonettes. Excavation in advance of the housebuilding produced a fairly complete plan of the N half of the fort, which had an area of about 2.4 acres (0.9 ha.) overall, with barracks and storebuildings, and a large stone-built granary, all of which lay scarcely 30cm below the lawns and shrubberies of the Victorian villas and had amazingly survived landscaping and terracing in the 1880s. The Antonine Wall itself, on the crest of the slope overlooking the Manse Burn, had been swept away, but the accompanying ditch was located, as were the E and W ramparts of the fort, and ditches beyond them. In an Annexe lying to the E was the fort bath-house, the discovery of which was the highlight of the excavations, and which has now been laid out as an ancient monument, though tightly hedged about by the modern development. (On Roman Road, 300m E of Bearsden Cross; AM signposts.) An information board provides a valuable, and colourful, guide to the layout of

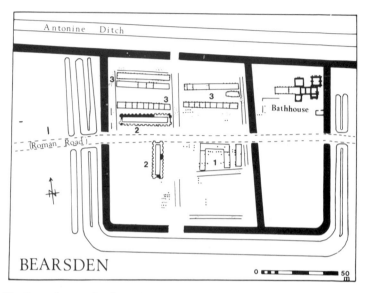

71. Bearsden on the Antonine Wall: ground-plan of the fort (after Breeze). Note: 1 = workshop(?), 2 = granaries, 3 = barracks and stores.

72. Excavation in progress at Bearsden bathhouse, 1979. (Photo: L. Keppie.)

73. **Head of a goddess**, perhaps Fortuna (Good Fortune), from Bearsden; about half life size. (Photo: Hunterian Museum.)

rooms. A timber-framed changing room led to a cold room and then to a sequence of heated compartments; opening separately off the cold room was a hot dry room, of which the floor is well preserved with a channelled hypocaust below and the furnace mouth beyond (Fig. 17). Opposite was a semicircular cold-plunge bath. A fine sandstone head of a goddess, sometimes identified as Fortuna (Good Fortune), was found in the plunge-bath in 1973. In the furthest heated room (the hot room) heat was directed up the walls not in the usual clay piping but behind thin stone slabbing kept clear of the walls by stone 'headers'. Just to the N are the walls of a room supported by buttresses. This was evidently a heated compartment, but it seems to have passed out of use early in the lifetime of the bath-house. Nearby to the SE is a small rectangular structure, identifiable as a latrine block. Analysis of sewage deposits in a nearby Annexe ditch brought the relevation that the soldiers' diet was primarily vegetarian, and had included raspberries, strawberries and figs, along with opium poppy and coriander seeds for flavouring bread.

South of Roman Road, within the grounds of Maxholme, now a Baptist Church, limited excavation in flowerbeds, under lawns and driveways, by permission of Bearsden and Milngavie District Council, revealed a second stone granary, and traces of other buildings including a workshop. The sharp fall away in the ground beyond the house marks the S limit of the fort. An inscribed building stone found near the stone-built granary N of Roman Road indicates that some part of the work was carried out by men of the Twentieth Legion.

To the W of Bearsden fort, the Wall continues due W across the A809 into gardens on the N side of **Thorn Road** (a short stretch of stone base discovered in one garden in 1973 has been laid out as a garden feature). Thereafter the Wall turned to the NW (some stonework can be seen in gardens in Colquhoun Drive and Milverton Avenue). A further turn to the W bought the frontier to a ridge where the course of the rampart and ditch is preserved in an area of grassland known as Roman Park (reached from **Ballaig Avenue**, where it joins Westbourne Crescent; look for a narrow path leading uphill opposite the house 'Four Wynds'; alternatively this stretch is accessible from the W, via Iain Road, by steps between nos. 85 and 87). The course of the Wall is defined on the ground by concrete markers. At the W end of the stretch an area of stone base cleared in 1963 lies exposed behind railings, though a matching ditch-section was backfilled in the 1970s. Further W the line of the Wall was left clear during housing developments in the 1960s (between Rosslyn Road and Antonine Road; AM signposts).

The Wall now climbs to the heights of **Castlehill**, surmounted by a circle of beech trees. (Just S of the A810, beyond the W outskirts of Bearsden; turn left off the A810, immediately after Antonine Road; park at a small telephone exchange, and walk uphill. The hedge-line straight ahead marks the course of the Antonine Wall running W towards the hill itself.) Older antiquarians believed that the fort lay entirely within the tree-circle, but aerial photography has shown that it lay partly on sloping ground to the E. No excavation has taken place on the hilltop, but when trees are blown over in a winter's gale pottery fragments are sometimes found in their roots. A small raised plateau at the NW corner of the hill, within the tree-circle, may mark the site of a mile-fortlet preceding the fort, and subsequently linked to its W defences (compare Duntocher, below, p. 141). Of the fort itself there is very little to see: a slight depression running S a little to the E of the raised plateau may mark the position of the W defences of the fort; the S defences lie a little beyond the field boundary on the S side of the hilltop. The garrison of the fort was at one time the Fourth Cohort of Gauls; an altar dedicated by its prefect and honouring the 'Goddesses of the Paradeground' (a favourite object of military veneration) was found there in 1826. From the summit the visitor can on a clear day see most of the Wall forts E to Bar Hill, and to the W the fort-site at Duntocher (though not Old Kilpatrick) is in view, along with those at Bishopton and Barochan on the far bank of the Clyde (above p. 97).

From Castlehill the Wall descends to the SW along a hedge-line,

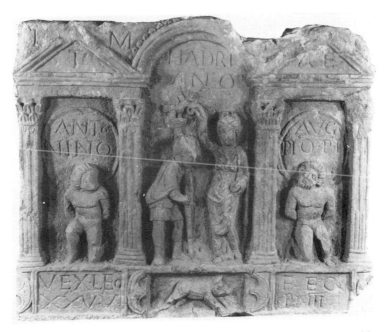

74. **Distance slab**, from Hutcheson Hill on the Antonine Wall, erected by men of the Twentieth Legion to record the completion of 3000 feet of the work; found in 1969. (Photo: Hunterian Museum.)

crossing Peel Glen Road to reach the Peel Burn. Beyond the Burn the Wall rises to cross Hutcheson Hill, its ditch scarcely visible except when low winter sunlight accentuates the hollow; then it descends to the Cleddans Burn on the outskirts of Drumchapel, with the ditch-hollow clearly visible flanked by thick gorse bushes. Just E of the Burn a magnificent distance slab was ploughed up in 1969. Beyond the Burn the ditch becomes visible again, as a dip close to the edge of a field, on the S side of a track leading to Cleddans farmhouse. On high ground beyond the farm – the only point in the two-mile stretch

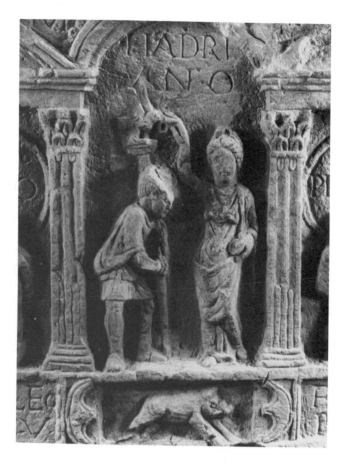

75. **Distance slab** from Hutcheson Hill on the Antonine Wall: central scene showing Britannia(?) in the act of presenting a laurel wreath to the Eagle of the Twentieth Legion held by its standard-bearer. (Photo: Hunterian Museum.)

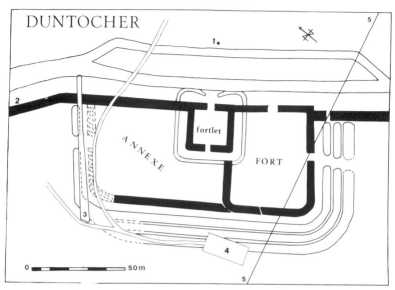

76. **Duntocher on the Antonine Wall**: ground-plan of the fortlet and fort (after Robertson). Note: 1 = flagpole, 2 = visible stretch of stone rampart-base, 3 = hedge, 4 = swings, 5 = boundary fence of housing development.

between Castlehill and Duntocher where both these fort-sites are simultaneously in view – a mile-fortlet was found by trial excavation in 1980. The Wall's course beyond Cleddans is overlaid by the modern farmtrack until it is lost in the edge of the much expanded village of **Duntocher**. Nothing can be seen until the Wall climbs to the summit of Golden Hill, which was the site of a small fort excavated in 1947–51 before the S half of the hilltop was built over by housing. The rest lies within a park. (From the A82 at a roundabout take the A8014 towards Duntocher; as it veers right at a garage, take Milton Douglas Road and its continuation, Roman Road; watch for the Antonine Sports Barn, and park opposite it at a church. A little beyond is a war memorial, from which a path leads up to the hilltop.) A short length of the Wall's stone base, left open after excavation in 1947, is displayed behind railings. It is sometimes very overgrown, and the culvert which crosses the base at a slant is hardly visible now; there is a much battered information board. This stretch of base provides a useful indicator of the Wall's alignment. Just to the S of its line, immediately behind the war memorial, part of the fort bath-house, originally discovered in 1775, was located again in 1978. In front of the stone base is a broad shallow hollow representing the ditch which can be followed uphill to the summit; but on the hilltop there is nothing for today's visitor to see. The earliest structure on the summit was a mile-fortlet, constructed in advance of the Wall itself. Initially examined in 1947–51, the fortlet's rampart was completely exposed in 1977–78, in the hope that it might become a permanent 'ancient monument'; but the trenches have now been backfilled. The fort itself was built to the E of the fortlet, incorporating the latter's E rampart in its defences.

Beyond Duntocher Burn – a slab on the bridge, erected in 1772 by Lord Blantyre, is often mistakenly identified as Roman because of its Latin inscription – the Wall, now increasingly overlooked by the Kilpatrick Hills, is lost again in the village of Duntocher, though the V-shape of the ditch could until recently be espied in the corrugated iron sheeting bounding a football pitch. Thereafter the Wall follows the line of Beeches Road, and then a bridle path, to pass in front of Carleith farm. West of Carleith it continues to follow a modern track towards a clump of trees; thereafter it is completely lost in farmland before rising to the farmhouse of Mount Pleasant. The hollow of the ditch was visible in the farmyard until destroyed by wartime bombing in 1941. Beyond Mount Pleasant the Wall descends to its terminus at Old Kilpatrick, its course cut by the A82 'boulevard' and then by housing. The fort site at Old Kilpatrick was excavated in 1923–24 prior to house-building. (Reached from the A82 by turning left, immediately after the access route to the Erskine Bridge, and then right on to the A814; stop in the village at a bus garage on the left; this overlies the N half of the fort.) Old Kilpatrick fort was quite large, 4.2 acres (1.7 ha.), and evidently built before the Wall builders arrived. The headquarters and a granary were in stone, with timber-framed stores and barracks to front and rear. In 1969 a splendid altar dedicated to Jupiter by the fort's garrison, the First Cohort of Baetasians, was found lying in one of the outer ditches on the NE side, during the digging of an inspection pit in garage premises N of the A814. The area between the fort and the River Clyde (reached by turning off the A814 into Gavinburn Place and then right into Portpatrick Road) contained the fort bath-house and other buildings, but it is now disfigured by the Forth & Clyde Canal. The splendid little canal bridge at Ferrydyke, between the fort-plateau and the river, marks the Wall's course as it approaches the Clyde. Sometime

77. **Altar to Jupiter**, from Old Kilpatrick on the Antonine Wall; found in 1969. It was erected by the First Cohort of Baetasians under their prefect Publicius Maternus. (Photo: Hunterian Museum.)

before 1684 a distance slab of the Twentieth Legion, showing a reclining figure of the goddess Victory holding a wreath to celebrate the success of the Roman army, was found at Ferrydyke cottages; it may have stood at the W terminus of the Wall. Another stone, probably a distance slab, was seen in the 1750s serving as a threshold in one of the cottages, but it has long since disappeared from view. For the Wall builders this was the end of 37 miles of building work.

CHAPTER 12

Scotland North of the Antonine Wall

A. From Forth to Tay

Just 1.5km N of the Antonine Wall, on the banks of the River Carron
and overlooking the Forth, lay the fort at **Camelon**, on a natural land
route to the N, between the Forth and the Kilsyth Hills. The plateau
occupied by the fort is now surrounded on three sides by a golf course,
and on the fourth by a railway line and factories. (To reach it, take the
A9 W out of Falkirk; after 1km look for a golf clubhouse on left; ask at
the clubhouse for permission to cross the course to the plateau behind,
which is fringed by hawthorn bushes; alternatively, continue N on the
A9 for a further 500m to an access road into the course beside a bus
garage. This road heads directly towards the plateau.) When the
plateau is reached, the fort-platform is easily discerned, with low
bankings representing the rampart on the W, N and E sides, with dips
in the bank marking gateways, most obviously on the E side. This was
the site of an Antonine fort, which had an area of 5.9 acres (2.4 ha.),
with internal buildings entirely of stone. The zone to the S, across the
railway, was very probably the site of the Flavian fort here (and later
an Antonine annexe); it was built over by factories at the turn of the
century. Recent development work has permitted excavation in 1975–
79, adding to our appreciation of the Flavian occupation. The significance of Camelon as a staging post for forces moving N–S in Roman
Scotland has been revealed over the years with the discovery from the
air of at least 10 temporary camps lying both W and S of the fort.

Three km N of Camelon there stood until 1743 a beehive-shaped
stone structure, over 6m in diameter and some 7m high, known from
mediaeval times as 'Arthur's O'on' (= Oven). The antiquarian writers
report sculptured figures on its outer facade, and in about 1700 the
single finger of a bronze statue was found inside. The precise function
of the O'on has not been established; we could most easily think of it
as a tomb, but some scholars have argued that it was a victory
monument, associated with the campaigns of Agricola, Lollius

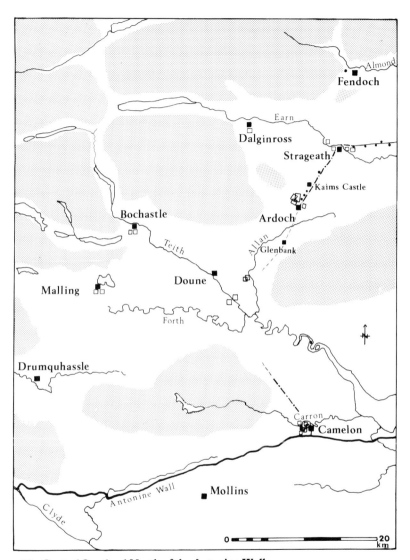

78. **Central Scotland North of the Antonine Wall.**

Urbicus or even Severus. A full-size replica, built in 1767, surmounts the stable block of Penicuik House, the former home of the antiquarian Sir John Clerk, where it can be seen today.

The Roman road continued from the N gate of Camelon fort

79. **Ardoch, Perthshire**: aerial view of the fort from the N, showing its ramparts and defensive ditches. (Photo: Colin Martin, by courtesy of the Department of Scottish History, University of St. Andrews.)

towards Stirling, but is scarcely visible except in woods NW of Torwood village. The precise point where the Roman road crossed the Forth has never been established, but camps have been found recently beside the river W of Stirling itself, and a fort of 6.3 acres (2.6 ha.) has been newly identified from the air at Doune, so that it seems possible now that the Romans' crossing-point lay much further W than hitherto supposed.

From the Forth the road continued NE up the valley of the Allan Water, past a newly found fortlet at Glenbank near Greenloaning, to Ardoch beside the River Knaik. **Ardoch★★** must rank as the single most impressive Roman fort in Scotland because of the fine state of preservation of its defences. (From the A9 at Greenloaning follow the A822 to Braco village; park on the N edge of the village, where the road veers to the right, and walk across a bridge to an access point at the fort's W gate where there is a tourist sign; alternatively there is a layby 150m beyond the bridge.) The rampart stands to a height of about 2m, and the ditches have a depth of over 2m, almost as left by the Romans 1800 years ago. (The visitor should walk round the ramparts in an anti-

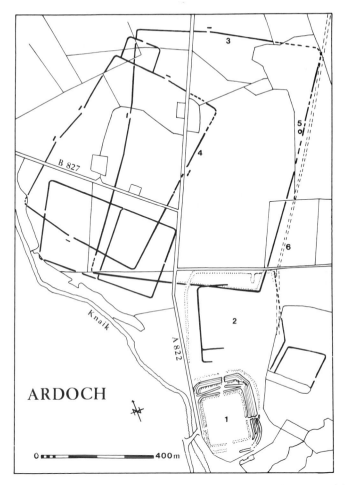

80. **Ardoch, Perthshire**: ground-plan of the fort and marching camps (after St. Joseph). Note: 1 = fort, 2 = annexe (within which are the ditches of a small camp), 3 = 130-acre (55ha.) camp, 4 = 63-acre (25ha.) camp, 5 = watch-tower in Blackhill Wood, 6 = Roman road northwards to Kaims Castle.

clockwise direction, stopping to admire the defences when he reaches the E gate. Walk out on to the causeway there to get the best view.) The multiplication of ditches (five in all) on the E and N sides is the result, it now seems, not of anxiety over the fort's security against attack, but of successive reductions in its size, as the garrison itself was cut back: the outer ditches on each side are the earliest, and the inner circuits were added later. The sequence is clearest on the N side of the fort (walk round now to the N gate), where stubs of the original rampart still stand, cut by the later ditches. The bank beyond the outer ditches is thought to be relatively modern. The W defences were destroyed by the modern road, and those on the S marred by cultivation. The fort, occupied in both Flavian and Antonine periods, was comprehensively excavated in 1896–97; the internal buildings seem to have been of timber in both periods, though a single barrack in stone was found. Nothing is visible of the internal arrangements – the enclosure in the middle of the fort is a mediaeval graveyard with a rectangular chapel at its centre. Initially the fort had an area of about 8.6 acres (3.5 ha.), but by the close of the Antonine period it had been reduced to about 5.7 acres (2.3 ha.).

Ardoch fort did not stand alone. To the N was an Annexe, of which the ramparts can be traced on the ground. Cutting through the N part of the Annexe are the defences of a large temporary camp of some 130 acres (55 ha.), perhaps belonging to Severus' campaigns, which overlie a small double-ditched watch-tower lying one Roman mile N of the fort. Other camps, including one of 63 acres (25 ha.), lie some distance from the fort to the NW. Parts of these installations survive in the heather-covered landscape around Ardoch, and were initially surveyed by General Roy; gaps in our knowledge have been filled over the years through aerial photography when the outlines of the camps have appeared as cropmarks in cultivated ground. It is perhaps best for the visitor who has drunk his fill of the fort-site to pass through the ditches on its N side by a causeway, and veer left to reach the A822 at a metal field gate. Here look right to see the defensive ditch of the Annexe, which should now be followed N for 300m across a fence into bracken-covered ground; here the ditch is accompanied by a 1.5m-high rampart bank. Just beyond the area of rough ground, the Annexe ditch cuts through the S rampart of the 130-acre camp. The Annexe ditch soon turns E to run along the S side of a minor road to Auchterarder. As the Annexe defences run E they become less and less impressive, and the line is obscured by modern bankings, until (just opposite a wooden gate on the far side of the Auchterarder road) the Annexe ditch seems to be cut through in turn by the ditch of the 130-acre camp.

Some further stretches of the rampart and ditch of both the 63-acre and 130-acre camps are to be seen, but interesting as these would be if found elsewhere, they could seem an anticlimax after the fort-defences themselves. To see the best of these, go N on the A822 to its junction with the B827 signposted for Comrie; about 50m along the secondary road, and just beyond a 'give way' sign, look at the sloping ground on the right to see a length of rampart of the 63-acre camp covered by heather. Some 200m further on, also on the right, there begins a long stretch of some 300m of the rampart and accompanying ditch of the 130-acre camp, running N–S. (Best reached by crossing from the previously visited stretch, passing behind a cottage to reach the boundary fence of an electricity substation.) The low banking of the rampart can be followed N across the heather-covered hillside; close to the far end is a break in the rampart, masked by a traverse. Some distance to the N can be seen a 250m-length of mound running E–W, which overlies the N rampart of the 63-acre camp. Most probably the visible mound is fairly modern (This stretch can also be seen from the A822, beginning 50m N of Blackhills cottage.) The Roman road going N from Ardoch was flanked by watch-towers at roughly one Roman mile intervals; four such towers are known, the nearest to Ardoch lying in Blackhill Wood where a circular mound can be vaguely discerned, though much obscured by woodland.

At **Kaims Castle****, about halfway between Ardoch and the next fort at Strageath, lies a fortlet, almost square in shape, c. 30m × 30m, within a single, almost circular ditch. (On the A822 3km N of Ardoch and 4km S of Muthill village, opposite the driveway to Orchill Home Farm; the fortlet lies in rough pasture W of the modern road, behind a cottage; go through a wooden farm gate S of the cottage; the fortlet lies 60m in front on a prominent knoll.) Kaims Castle is among the best-preserved fortlets in Scotland, with the rampart still standing to a height of over 1.5m, and the ditch 3m wide and 1m deep with an upcast mound beyond. There was a single gate, on the E side, facing the Roman road, which was reached by means of a causeway across the ditch. The road itself can be seen as a faint ridge passing across the front of the fortlet halfway between its ditch and the modern highway. The interior of the fortlet, excavated in 1900, was paved with cobbles, surely in a secondary phase, but no structures were located or small finds made.

Some 6km further N is the next fort, at **Strageath**, overlooking the river Earn. (From the A822 at Muthill where the main road turns to the left at Muthill Old Church and Tower, go right and then left at a sign 'Strageath 2'; turn right again almost immediately and follow the road for 3km to Strageath Mains Farm. Park at the farmhouse and request access. The fort lies on the plateau to the S. Go uphill along a field boundary marked with trees from the front of the farm buildings, then left along another tree-lined fence. About 120m into this second field note the low bank which represents the rampart of an annexe; some 80m further on is the fort-platform, with the rampart surviving as a low mound; continue along the fence which turns right and then left.) The second fence-corner lies atop the N rampart of the fort, which can be seen turning the NE angle. Aerial photography over many years has revealed the outlines of a complex ditch-system. Excavation from 1973 onwards under the auspices of the Scottish Field School of Archaeology has established a detailed plan of much of the N half of the fort; small finds have included a 'pig' of lead and some scale-armour. The fort was in use in both Flavian and Antonine periods. Its importance came from its position guarding the crossing of the Earn.

Beyond Strageath the Roman road continues to the N to cross the river near Innerpeffray (where there are two temporary camps), then turns E to ascend the **Gask Ridge**, an E–W spine of land N of the Earn with fine views N towards Glenalmond, as well as back into the hollow of Strathearn. Where it passed along the Gask Ridge the road was flanked by watch-towers at roughly one-mile intervals; ten or eleven sites are known, placed a little way to one or other side of the road. Several, long known to antiquarians, were excavated in 1900; others have been located more recently through aerial photography. The towers were of a standard plan: about 3m square, with substantial timber uprights at the four corners, probably supporting a structure two or (better) three storeys high. Each tower was enclosed by a rampart and a single ditch, with a gap to allow access from the road. The spoil from the ditch was used to form a low counterscarp bank. Seven of the towers are visible today, in varying degrees of impressiveness; those most worth visiting are at Parkneuk, Kirkhill and Muir O' Fauld. The visitor should not underestimate the time needed to find some of the sites in dense woodland, though recent work by the Historic Buildings and Monuments Division of the Scottish Development Department has made access easier at several sites. The line of the Roman road can be followed on foot from Ardunie farm to Midgate, though the view to N and S is often obscured by forestry.

At the W end of the Ridge above the Earn crossing is the watch-tower at **Parkneuk**★ (see Fig. 20). (Reached by taking the B8062 from Crieff or from Auchterarder; 2.5km N of Kinkell Bridge, the road

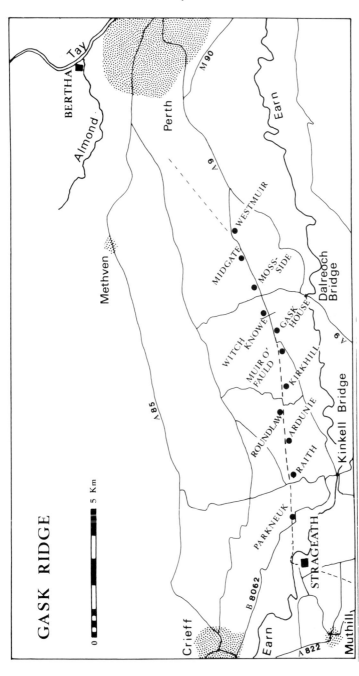

81. **Gask Ridge, Perthshire**, showing sequence of watch-towers.

F

swings sharply to the left at some woodland; look for an access road into the wood and park there; pass through a wooden gate, and 50m beyond, turn sharply right to see the watch-tower in rough grassland c. 50m beyond, somewhat overgrown by bracken.) The ground plan was established by excavation in 1968. The ditch is now 3.5m wide and 0.75m deep, with the counterscarp bank prominent. Little is preserved of the rampart, but there is a causeway across the ditch to the N to reach the road itself which survives in the woodland as a low cambered mound 30m in front. Walking back to the modern road, the visitor should stop at the wooden gate, and look forward c. 10m to left and right, to see a prominent bank which constitutes the N rampart of the larger of two temporary camps lying beside the Earn at Innerpeffray; the accompanying ditch is on the woodland side of the bank.

To see other towers of the Gask Ridge system, the visitor should go via Kinkell Bridge to Trinity Gask, then follow signs to Madderty; 700m N of the Trinity Gask Church the road swings sharply E to follow the Roman highway. From this point the visitor can walk W for 1.3km to the site of **Ardunie** tower (AM signpost), but it is poorly preserved. More profitably, follow the Roman road E from this point into woodland, past a gate and over a plantation bank; at a clearing 50m beyond, look for a path on the right to the watch-tower of **Kirkhill★**, where a circular ditch 0.5m deep, broken by a causeway, enclosed the platform where the tower once stood. (Permission to visit this site must be sought from the estate factor, at nearby Lawhill.) The Roman road can be followed E on foot along the spine of the ridge to **Muir O' Fauld★** tower. (The motorist needs to return to Trinity Gask, turn left and continue for 3km; where the road swings to the left and then sharp right, the line of the Roman road is again reached. This point can also be reached from the old A9 at Dalreoch Bridge, signposted Findo Gask.) Park at the double bend in the road, and walk W past a locked metal gate for 350m. An AM arrow on the left guides the visitor to the tower, now enclosed within a new fence and sturdy gate. All the constituent features are visible here: a low rampart within its surrounding ditch, broken by a causeway N to the road, and counterscarp bank beyond.

Return now to the modern highway; some 500m E of the double bend, another tower, named **Gask House**, lies in dense woodland to the S of the road. (Look for an ungated fire-break with fire-danger sign; then walk a further 80m along the road to the E, and pass through a break in the fence to reach the tower, c. 20m into the woods.) The ditch is well preserved. The next tower in the sequence, at **Witch Knowe**, is overgrown, but repays a visit. (Continue E to the lodge-cottage at Gask House, then walk E for c. 120m to a gap in the woodland on the N side of the road; aim for the far left corner of the clearing, c. 180m from the road; the tower is a further 30m on, within a broken-down fence.) The ditch has a depth of 0.5m with a counter-scarp bank beyond. The site of another tower can be viewed at **Midgate**, a further 2.5km to the E atop a natural hillock. (Opposite the unsignposted access road to Blairbell; climb on to a hillock E of a metalled farm track but W of a second hillock topped by brick structures.) The ditch of the tower is poorly represented by a hollow 0.25m deep, its course marked by thistles, enclosing an area c. 12m square overall. Doubtless other towers remain to be discovered eastwards towards the Tay. The precise context in which these towers were built is not totally certain: excavation at Gask House tower in 1965 produced a small fragment of *mortarium* rim (above, p. 54), dated to the period c. AD 70–95, which has been used to date the system to the Flavian period. Scholars have seen the system of towers N of Ardoch and along the Gask Ridge as a patrolled frontier line, perhaps belonging to the time when forts N of the Earn were abandoned (c. 85–90 AD), making the Gask Ridge in effect the N limit of the Roman province. But some confirmation of the dating would be welcome before too many hypotheses are constructed.

The valley of the Earn was traversed by Roman troops from the time of Agricola onwards: camps of about 115 acres (46.5 ha.) at Dunning and Abernethy are dated to this time, and another member of the same series is suspected S of the Severan fortress at Carpow. Part of the N side of the camp-defences at **Dunning** can be seen in Kincladie wood. (0.8km N of Dunning on the B934; begin at the roadside c. 80m from the SW corner of the wood, where the B934 tops a small rise.) The rampart stands 0.6m high with a ditch to its right, extending into the wood for 130m; the modern road passes through a gateway in the camp defences. The gap was masked by a traverse c. 15m in front of the rampart. The traverse is still visible close up against the modern fence beside the road.

Carpow, perhaps the place named *Orrea* by the geographer Ptolemy, lies just E of the junction between the Earn and the Tay, with extensive views across the Firth. (In open farmland, north of the A913, 3km W of Newburgh; for access to the site, ask at Carpow

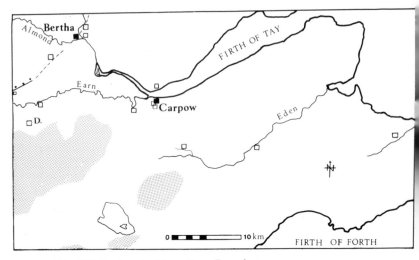

82. **The Fife Peninsula**. Note: D. = Dunning.

House.) An old tradition of Roman antiquities was confirmed in 1961–62; excavation has continued intermittently ever since. The fortress, of some 30 acres (12 ha.), was set within a rampart and double ditch. The gates were stone-built: two have yielded fragments of stone commemorative tablets (now in Dundee Museum). The inscription on the E gate slab has been restored to show a dedication to the emperor Caracalla, presumably in AD 211–212, shortly before the final Roman withdrawal from Scotland; sculptured motifs include emblems of the Second Legion *Augusta*, which is thus identified as the builder. Within the fortress, excavation has revealed the headquarters building and a commanding officer's mansion; roofing tiles here bear the name of the Sixth Legion, with an added title *Britannica*, which it apparently acquired in AD 210–211. A granary in stone, or on stone foundations, was also explored, and some trial work has been done on one area of barracks which were of timber. Carpow fortress could have housed about 3000 men. Little can be seen today, but the ripple of the S defences can be made out in the fields E of Carpow House, and in drought conditions the lines of ditches on the E and S sides of the fortress are visible to the passer-by from the adjacent A913.

In the interior of Fife, a map of some 20 years ago would have shown no Roman sites, but three are now known, probably indicating that the Romans penetrated into Fife by the central E–W route with

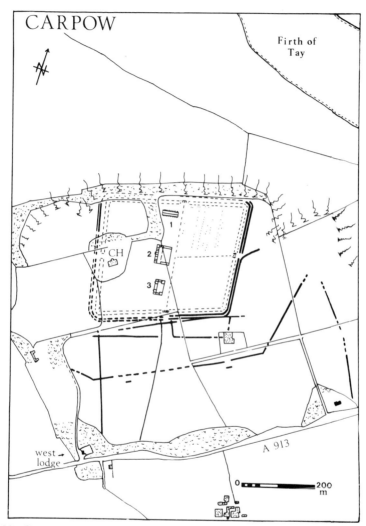

83. **Carpow, Perthshire**: ground-plan of the fortress and marching camps (after St. Joseph and Wilkes). Note: 1 = granary, 2 = headquarters, 3 = residence of legion's commander; CH = Carpow House.

the Ochil Hills on the one side and the Lomond Hills on the other, reaching and following the River Eden to its mouth in St. Andrews Bay where a fort would not now be completely unexpected. Doubtless, too, Roman forces followed the S coast of the Fife peninsula, but no sites are known there as yet.

84. **Carpow, Perthshire**: aerial view of the Severan fortress from the NE. Note the broad ditches on the E and S sides, a road issuing from the E gateway, and small rubbish pits (seen as dots) providing a clue to the general layout of internal buildings. (Photo: RCAHMS.)

B. The Highland Line Forts

West of the Roman road from the Forth to the Tay is a group of forts placed by Agricola or his immediate successor at the mouths of various Highland glens (see Fig. 78). Most scholars believe that they were intended to prevent access to Roman-held territory by the tribesmen of the mountains beyond. The best known is at **Fendoch** (see Fig. 16), close to the mouth of the Sma' Glen, where the river Almond issues from a narrow defile and descends into Strathalmond. (For the traveller from the S, the easiest approach is from Crieff, turning off the A85 on to the A822 at Gilmerton; look for the junction of the A822 with the B8063; park at the AA telephone beside the junction.) The fort itself lay on a levelled platform 500m to the SE, slightly back from the entrance to the Sma' Glen, with a range of hills behind it. On the ground today a faint ridge marks the line of the ramparts, and the hollow of a ditch can be made out at the SW corner of the fort. The site was excavated by Sir Ian Richmond in 1936–38, and its ground plan is well known; the fort probably housed an 800-strong regiment of auxiliary infantry.

On high ground W of the modern road into the Glen, c. 350m N of the AA box, lies a watch-tower. (Look for the *third* hillock from the modern road; a narrow path leads to the summit.) This tower (**Sma' Glen★**) was the 'eye' of Fendoch, with a splendid forward view into the Glen, and within easy view of the fort to pass back information about hostile activity. The rampart is set within a single ditch, which is broken by an entrance on the SE side facing the fort. From the watch-tower the visitor can easily appreciate the purpose of the fort itself, a cork in the mouth of the Sma' Glen.

Some 18km to the SW (and best reached from Crieff along the A85) was the fort of **Dalginross** (see Fig. 14), first surveyed by William Roy in 1755, at the head of Strathearn. The fort site (W of the B827 on the S outskirts of Comrie, by Dalginross farm) is partly eroded by the adjacent river, but its platform is easily made out, and a slight roll in the ground betrays the position of the ditches. Lying next to it (and straddling the modern road) was a 23.5-acre (9.5-ha.) camp of the Stracathro type, also surveyed by Roy, which has since been relocated from the air (see Fig. 14).

Further again to the SW, at **Bochastle★** on the outskirts of Callander, was another Highland Line fort, just below the Pass of Leny, where the River Teith emerges into open country. (Turn off the A84 2km W of Callander on to the A821; just across the river take a farm track on the left at the 'picnic area' and drive as far as (but not under) the bridge below a now disused railway; climb on to the railway embankment for an elevated view of the fort which lies between the embankment and the river.) The W rampart survives as a broad bank up to 2.7m high, with a gap for the W gate. The N rampart has been eroded by the river, and the S rampart partly lost below the embankment, but the E rampart and ditches are visible. The fort was about 6 acres (2.4 ha.) in size; excavation in 1949 established a Flavian date, and showed that the site had suffered from flooding even in Roman times. On the S side of the fort were two camps, one with a Stracathro gateway.

The next Highland Line fort was at Malling, on the S shore of the Lake of Menteith, in the upper valley of the Forth, with the Menteith Hills and Ben Ledi rising sharply in front. The fort, which is of some 7 acres (2.8 ha.), with an annexe on the lochside, was found from the air in the later 1960s. Near to it were two camps, of which one has a Stracathro-type gate. (A short length of ditch belonging to the larger of the two camps survives next to a forestry plantation, but makes for a disappointing visit.)

Finally there was a fort near Drymen at Drumquhassle farm close by the Endrick Water above Loch Lomond, on high ground with fine all-round views, bounded by mountains of the Highland massif on the N, the Kilpatrick Hills to the S, and on the SE by the distinctive summit of Dumgoyne at the end of the Campsie range. The fort was of about 3.2 acres (1.43 ha.); its ramparts are visible as a rather low mound, discernible only to the experienced observer. A final fort in the series, completing the cordon, could be looked for on the banks of the Leven, at or near Dumbarton.

C. From the Tay to the North Esk

The fort at **Bertha**, the jumping-off point for Roman incursions into Strathmore, sat at the junction between the Tay and the Almond, 3km north of Perth. (Take the A9 out of Perth to the N; after crossing the Almond, turn immediately left into a cul-de-sac. The fort lies in the field opposite, beyond the A9, and is bisected by the railway. A faint ridge representing the N rampart lies directly ahead, silhouetted against the railway embankment; a short length of what seems to be the S rampart survives in woodland overlooking the Almond on the margin of cultivated ground, beyond the railway line). The fort was large, about 9.5 acres (3.8 ha.). In 1958 a dedication stone to *Discipulina Augusti*, the military discipline-cult favoured by emperors from Hadrian onwards, was recovered from the bed of the Almond nearby and is now in Perth Museum.

For Roman troops advancing north-eastwards from the Tay, two possible routes were available, either along the coast S of the Sidlaw Hills or through Strathmore following the Tay itself and its various tributaries to the NE. It is evident that the Roman army used both. Two series of camps, already referred to (above, p. 28), stand out: of

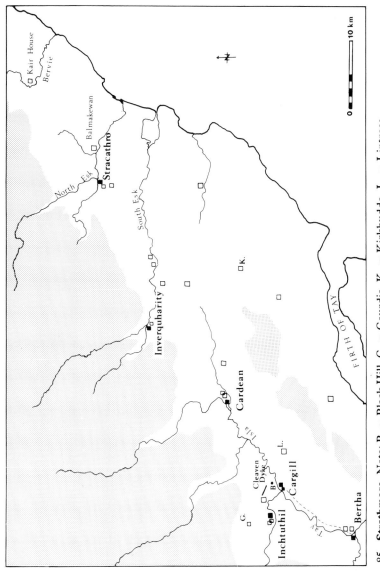

85. **Strathmore.** Note: B. = Black Hill, G. = Gourdie, K. = Kirkbuddo, L. = Lintrose.

G

63 and 130 acres (25 and 55 ha.), evidently indicating the progress of particular task-forces, most probably in the Severan period. Just beyond Bertha, on the far side of the Tay, two such camps are known, at Scone and Grassy Walls, the former of 63 acres and the latter of 130. Some parts of the ramparts of the Grassy Walls camp are visible as faint mounds.

Impressive lengths of the rampart and ditch of a 63-acre (25-ha.) camp can be seen at **Kirkbuddo***, S of Forfar. (On the B9127, 5km E of its junction with the A929 at Gateside; c. 1km E of the Whigstreet hamlet, the road veers to the left; park here on the right at a half-concealed wooden gate leading into woodland. On the *opposite* side of the road, 20m E of the gate, is the bank of the camp-rampart.) The rampart, 1.5m high with an accompanying ditch forming the W side of the camp, extends into the plantation for 300m. The rampart is broken by two gateways, each protected by a traverse c. 15m in front of the camp-ditch. The first gateway lies 100m into the plantation, the second c. 140m further on in open heather-covered ground beyond a zone of newly planted conifers. Both traverses are most impressive, consisting of a 12m length of rampart fronted by a ditch of matching length. (Next return to the B9127, and cross it to visit the continuation of the W side of the camp, which can be followed to the SW corner and then along the S side; shortly before the B9127 again comes into view is another gateway, with traverse.)

On the line of the Tay itself (and this was evidently the chief route used by the Romans when this part of Scotland was occupied in the later first century AD) there is a fort *and* a fortlet close together at Cargill, at the junction of the Tay and the Isla. The fortlet has been known since 1941; the fort was first located from the air in 1977. Both seem likely to belong in the Flavian period, given that the Romans do not seem to have established permanent forts N of the Tay in any other period. A particular problem must be to relate them chronologically to the major site in the area, indeed the kingpin of the whole Flavian system in Scotland, the legionary fortress at **Inchtuthil**, barely 5km distant to the NW.

The Inchtuthil fortress, first recognised as a major site in the 1750s, was examined in 1901 and comprehensively excavated in 1952–65; aerial reconnaisance over the years has added further details and confirmed the general correctness of the published plan which forms the most completely known ground plan of a legionary fortress

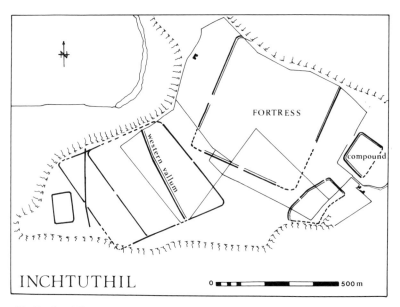

86. Inchtuthil, Perthshire: ground-plan of the fortress and adjacent enclosures (after St. Joseph). See Fig. 21 for a detailed plan of the fortress.

anywhere in the Roman Empire. The fortress, of 53 acres (21.5 ha.), was abandoned while still under construction in about AD 86/87, when the occupying legion (probably the Twentieth) was moved to Chester, and the garrison of Britain substantially reduced.

The site lies in a bend of the Tay at Caputh, just short of the Tay gorge at Dunkeld. (From the A984 W of Meikleour village, turn left on to a rough track opposite the junction with the B947; continue to the far end of the track beside some cottages. The fortress lies on the plateau above, and is reached along a path leading uphill to the right of the cottages.) On the right of the path within a plantation of rhododendrons are the rampart and defensive ditch of a rectangular enclosure, interpreted as a 'stores compound', somewhat disfigured by its use in cross-country equestrian courses. Some 100m into the field beyond is the broad E ditch of the fortress, which can be followed N (to the right) to an escarpment, on whose crest the N rampart lay (not now visible). The visitor should head W aiming for a white house in the distance, and just before a modern plantation bank he will encounter the fortress's W rampart, a broad low mound, running away to the left, its course marked by some trees. The accompanying

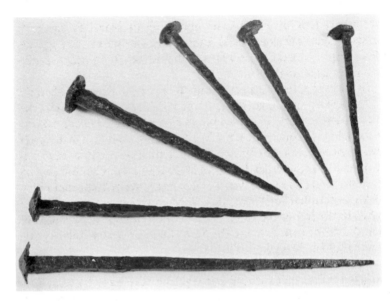

87. **Inchtuthil, Perthshire**: iron nails found below the workshop. The longest nail measures 32 cms. (Photo: Hunterian Museum.)

W ditch can be followed towards the SW corner where the remains peter out in a cultivated field. An impressive length of the S defences, comprising rampart, berm and ditch, is visible in a patch of rough ground nearby. Looking back to the E rampart, the visitor will gain an impression of the area covered by the fortress.

Rather disappointingly perhaps, there is nothing to be seen in the interior of the site (Fig. 21). The internal structures were timber-built, and included a headquarters building, hospital, workshop (from below the floor of which came the hoard of nearly 1,000,000 unused iron nails, left behind when the fortress was abandoned), and 64 barracks. Occasional bumps and hollows in the interior are remnants of a golf course, now disused. The rampart was initially of clay, but later received a stone revetment, left unfinished on the abandonment of the site. Close by, between the fortress and the end of the promontory on which it stands, was a labour camp and to the SE a temporary compound for officers, in use while the fortress was under construction. Ploughing regularly brings up débris from a bath-house which stood within the compound. Later, the whole promontory S of the fortress was cut off by the digging of a new rampart and ditch, the 'western vallum' of which some traces can be seen. (From the S rampart, walk NW along a field fence to reach a modern track; go left till a sharp dip marks the position of the Roman ditch which can be seen running off to the S.)

To the NW of Inchtuthil was a temporary camp at Gourdie. Within its limits is a group of large pits in the hillside, known locally as the 'Steed Stalls', a name which is sometimes applied to the site. It used to be thought that a quarry here produced building stone for the fortress's revetment wall, but the chief source of building stone is now known to lie some way to the W, and the date of the Steed Stalls has been called into question. (To see the Steed Stalls, return from Inchtuthil to the A984, and go left for 900m, then right to Gourdie farm; continue uphill to the top of the ridge beside farm buildings of Craigend of Gourdie farm; look E to see the Steed Stalls as grassy hillocks in a planted field c. 300m downhill.)

Some 3km E of Inchtuthil is a turf-revetted earthen bank flanked by shallow ditches which run in a straight line for some 2.25km. It is known as the **Cleaven Dyke**.* Its purpose and date have never been clear, but it could be seen as a Roman boundary line, marking one edge of the *territorium legionis*, i.e. the land directly under the legion's control where crops were grown and animals pastured to augment the food supply. (To see a length of the Dyke, take the minor road signposted Lethendy just W of Meikleour village; after 1km, where the woodland peters out on the right, follow its edge NE for 200m, until a bank and flanking ditches come into view straight ahead. Alternatively, the Dyke can be seen to either side of the A93, 700m N of its junction with the A984). There are two gaps in the dyke: seemingly overlooking the gaps at Meikleour is a watch-tower, atop a natural hillock known as **Black Hill** (see Fig. 20) because of the dark shadow cast by the thickly planted trees on its summit. (Reached from the A93 S of Meikleour, turning E on to an unsignposted track to Bridge farm; the watch-tower lies in the second field E of the farm.) Excavation in 1939 revealed a timber tower 3.5m square within a rampart and a single ditch, of which some faint traces remain. In the valley of the Isla, there is a camp of 63 acres (25 ha.) at Lintrose, 6km E of Cargill; its once impressive ramparts have largely fallen victim to agricultural improvement, though a short stretch survives in woodland on the N edge of the hamlet of Campmuir.

Further up the valley of the Isla, which continues the line of the Tay to the NE, is a fort (and two camps – the larger of 130 acres) at

Cardean, in the angle between the Isla and a tributary, the Dean Water. The fort belongs in the Flavian period; excavation in 1968–75 revealed a turf-built rampart with up to four external ditches; inside the fort the excavators located a timber-framed barrack block, a row of storerooms, and a granary; the foundation-trenches and pits for the major timber uprights showed up clearly in the yellow sandy subsoil. Only the general outlines of the fort are visible today. (From the A94 outside Meigle to the NW, take the A927 for Alyth, then almost immediately a minor road signposted Kirriemuir; soon after the road swings to the right to cross the Dean Water, look right at a farm gate to the plateau once occupied by the fort.)

The forts N from the Tay were linked by a road, along the line of the Isla. Just beyond Kirriemuir, in **Caddam Wood**, there is a fine stretch of cambered mound, which seems likely to be a remnant of this road, though some scholars have questioned its Roman date. (Follow the B955 out of Kirriemuir to the NE, turn left into Mid Road, opposite a bus stop; park at the end of the lane on the edge of the wood, and follow the track straight forward into the wood; after c. 50m the cambered surface of the road comes into view on the right-hand side, flanked by drainage ditches. The mound is topped by a tree. It can be followed to the NE, where it is joined by a modern track which continues for 500m through the wood.)

The line of Roman advance to the NE has always been supposed to cross the South Esk at Finavon, more or less on the line of the modern A94, where three camps are known, and a fort has been for some time postulated there. However, in 1983 aerial reconnaissance revealed a small fort, not at the expected river crossing on the South Esk, but 8km further W at Inverquharity Castle, at the junction of the South Esk with the Prosen Water and close to the mouths of Glen Clova and Glen Prosen. A Flavian date can be presumed, and Inverquharity fort can be seen as another in the 'Highland Line' series, to be divorced from the group of camps further E on the South Esk, which are on the main line of Roman advance northwards.

Further N at Stracathro, on the North Esk (where the river is met by two tributaries), lies what is currently the most northerly known fort in the Roman Empire, of some 6 acres (2.42 ha.), revealed initially by aerial reconnaissance, and confirmed as of Flavian date by limited excavation in 1969. The site is partly covered by Stracathro Church and churchyard. (Turn off the A94 4km N of Brechin to Westerton farm; after crossing one of the tributaries, turn right at a T-junction,

88. **Stracathro, Angus**: marching camp (centre left) and beyond it the Flavian fort (underlying the Church), seen from the S. (Photo: RCAHMS.) See also Fig. 13.

passing Smiddyhill farm, to reach Stracathro Church; park at the church gate.) The fort defences on the fort's E side can be made out in the field opposite the church gate. Close by to the W is a marching camp of just under 40 acres (15.7 ha.), the type-site of the Stracathro series (Fig. 13).

D. Aberdeenshire and the North

Beyond the North Esk no forts are securely known, but we should not suppose that Stracathro fort was necessarily the most northerly ever built in Scotland. Others may await detection from the air, perhaps at

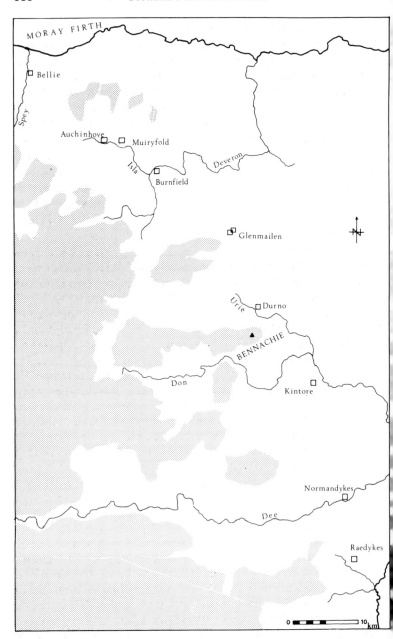

89. **Aberdeenshire and the North**.

Fordoun on the Bervie Water, where there has been a long tradition of Roman earthworks, and near Stonehaven. Certainly the discovery of numerous camps over the years indicates the onward march of Roman armies beyond the North Esk. At first the camps lie at fairly regular intervals about 16km apart, often at river crossings: Balmakewan on the far side of the North Esk (123 acres/49.7 ha.), Kair House (130 acres/52.6 ha.) on the Bervie Water; Raedykes (93 acres/37.6 ha.), Normandykes on the Aberdeenshire Dee (107 acres/ 43.3 ha.) and Kintore (110 acres/44.5 ha.) at the crossing of the Don. All these camps have been known for some time. The first two seem likely to belong to the series of 130-acre camps which stretch northwards from Ardoch and may belong in the Severan age. But those beyond Stonehaven are smaller and it is tempting to see them as a separate group, perhaps marking the progress of Agricola himself.

At **Raedykes**★ almost the entire ditch circuit can be followed on the ground. (5km NW of Stonehaven, turn N off the A957 at Mowtie on to a minor road, then fork right and where the road turns sharply right, go straight ahead on a track to Broomhill farm; as the farm is approached, the E rampart and ditch of the camp come into view on the right side of the track.) The E rampart stands up to 1m high and c. 3m broad, with a ditch beyond still up to 1m deep. Just opposite the farm buildings is a traverse ditch protecting a gateway; there is a second traverse about halfway between the farm and the camp's NE corner. The rampart should now be followed to the NE corner, where it runs sharply to the W. Here the defences are at their most impressive. After the second field boundary, at a slight change in alignment, there is another traverse. The ditch can be followed for much of the rest of the camp's outline, except where it is faint on the S side. The ground is very uneven hereabouts, with a steep hill in the middle of the site, which may help to account for the irregularity of the outline. The chief reason for the selection of this site must have been the fine vista over the long stretch of coastline, with the harbour of Stonehaven in full view.

Part of the N side of the camp at **Normandykes** survives along the edge of a forestry plantation, with the rampart standing 2m high, and the accompanying ditch 4m wide. (At Peterculter on the A93 SW of Aberdeen take a minor road to the SW past a mill and continue beside an old railway embankment; park at a track leading S towards the embankment, and then cross a stream to reach the plantation which stands clearly on the opposite slope; the nearer (left) corner of the plantation marks the NE angle of the Roman camp.)

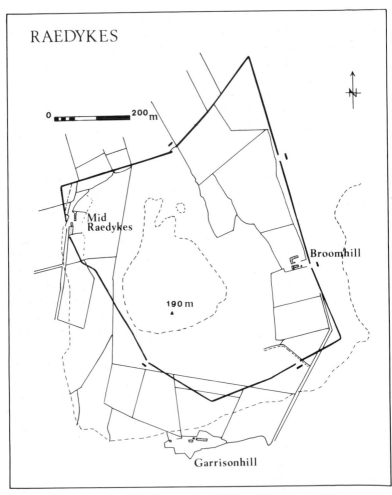

RAEDYKES

0 ▭▭▭▭ 200 m

N

Mid
Raedykes

Broomhill

190 m
▲

Garrisonhill

90. Raedykes, Aberdeenshire: ground-plan of the marching camp (after Macdonald).

Further N the line of Roman advance lay along the Don and subsequently its tributary, the River Urie. At Durno near Pitcaple, 10km NW of Inverurie, is a camp of 144 acres (58.2 ha.), revealed from the air in 1977. Nothing is visible at ground level. Although the camp, the largest N of the Forth, is undated, a persuasive case has been made out by Professor St. Joseph for identifying it as Agricola's base on the eve of the battle of *Mons Graupius*, which (it is suggested) was fought out on the slopes of Bennachie, 5km to the SW (above, p. 11). The conspicuous silhouette of Bennachie would make an excellent *Mons Graupius*, all but in sight of the 'end of Britain', as Tacitus reports. Although the camp at Durno is on the other side of the Urie river from Bennachie (Tacitus' account mentions no river barrier), it is sited at just a sufficient distance from the mountain to have discouraged overnight raiding from the Caledonian host encamped on its slopes. Yet it is too soon to regard the identification as proved.

Further to the NW two camps are known E of Huntly at **Glenmailen**. The defences of the larger camp of 111 acres (44.9 ha.) cut the rampart and ditch of the smaller which has a Stracathro-type gate. Evidently we have here evidence of *two* Roman armies, of greatly differing strength, using the same halting place. We could think of Agricolan forces in successive years (i.e. AD 82 and 83), unless this was an old Agricolan overnight encampment chosen again by Severus' army – all of 130 years later(!). The larger camp seems to belong with the group already mentioned (above, p. 167). (From the A96 23km N of Inverurie go right to Wells of Ythan, then 2km E on a minor road; park at Glenmailen farm. Cross the road, and then a dried-up stream bed; look for the boundary fence immediately in line with the stream bed as it descends the hillside opposite, and two field boundaries SW of Glenmailen farm itself.) Part of the S rampart of the larger camp survives along this field boundary, and other short stretches can with difficulty be pinpointed along its circuit.

The rampart of the Glenmailen camp is the most northerly surviving Roman earthwork in Britain, but beyond Glenmailen a further camp has been tentatively identified at Burnfield near Milltown on the river Deveron. Two more camps, located by aerial photography in the 1950s, lie close together near Keith, at Muiryfold and Auchinhove, where the River Isla negotiates the Pass of Grange. The camp at Auchinhove, of 30 acres (12 ha.), has Stracathro gates, and must be assigned to the Flavian period. The larger is of 109 acres (44.1 ha.). Here two task-forces have stopped at much the same halting place, a day's northwards march beyond Glenmailen. Some 20km beyond there is a possible camp (never confirmed as Roman by excavation) at Bellie NW of Fochabers, on a plateau above the flood-plain of the Spey at a point long used as a crossing over the river – it was here that part of the Duke of Cumberland's army crossed the Spey on its march to Culloden in 1746. That this camp (if confirmed) should mark the limit of Roman advances in Scotland must be highly unlikely;

certainly a further day's march would bring an army to Burghead, later an important Pictish fort. It is tempting to see in Burghead the *Pinnata Castra* ('winged' or 'battlemented camp') mentioned by Ptolemy, as lying on or near the Spey. Recent claims to have identified one or more Roman installations W of the Spey near Nairn have not yet been substantiated, but the idea of permanent installations N of the Grampians should not be too hastily rejected. Both Agricola and Severus are said to have reached the far end of Britain; whether such statements should be interpreted literally is for future researchers to determine.

Museums in Scotland with Roman Displays

(Intending visitors are advised to check opening hours with individual museums)

Bo'ness Kinneil Museum, Kinneil Estate (1st May–31st Oct: Mon.–Fri., 10 a.m.–12.30 p.m; 1.30 – 5 p.m; Sat., 10 a.m.–5 p.m; Nov.–Mar: Sat. only, 10 a.m.–5 p.m.). Finds from nearby Kinneil fortlet; altar from Westerwood fort.

Clydebank Old Town Hall, Dumbarton Road (Mon., Wed., 2–5 p.m., Sat., 10 a.m.–5 p.m.). Small display of local material.

Cumbernauld Cumbernauld Museum, Ardenlea House, The Wynd, Cumbernauld Village. (Thu. only, 2–8 p.m; other times by arrangement). Local finds, models and photographs.

Dumfries Dumfries Burgh Museum, The Observatory (Mon.–Sat., 10 a.m.–1 p.m. and 2–5 p.m; Sun. (April to September only), 2–5 p.m.). Good-sized display of altars from Birrens and small finds from Durisdeer, Carzield, Burnswark, Birrens and other sites in SW Scotland; activity sheets for school pupils.

Dundee McManus Galleries, Albert Square (Mon.–Sat., 10 a.m.–5 p.m.). Material from Carpow, including fragments of commemorative slabs.

Edinburgh Royal Museum of Scotland (formerly National Museum of Antiquities of Scotland), Queen St. (Mon.–Sat., 10 a.m.–5 p.m; Sun. 2–5 p.m.). Major permanent display, including altars, commemorative slabs, sculptures, and spectacular small finds from numerous sites, including Newstead, Birrens, Rough Castle, Mumrills, Fendoch. Also 'Traprain Treasure' (late 4th-century silver, loot from southern Britain). Guidebook and leaflets; slides.

Edinburgh City Museums, Huntly House, Canongate (Mon.–Sat., 10 a.m.–5 p.m; open till 6 p.m., June–Sept; Sun., 2–5 p.m. during Edinburgh Festival). Many interesting finds from Cramond fort.

Falkirk Falkirk Museum, 15 Orchard St. (Mon.–Sat., 10 a.m.–12.30 p.m., 1.30–5 p.m.). Local finds from sites in Falkirk District. Guidebook to local sites.

Glasgow Hunterian Museum, University of Glasgow (Mon.–Fri., 9.30 a.m.–5 p.m; Sat., 9.30 a.m.–1 p.m.). Major permanent display of material from Antonine Wall and sites in SW Scotland, including numerous distance slabs, and many small finds from forts at Bar Hill, Bearsden, Castledykes, Loudoun Hill and elsewhere; Roman coins. Guidebooks; teachers' packs; slides.

Glasgow Glasgow Art Gallery and Museum, Kelvingrove (Mon.–Sat., 10 a.m.–5 p.m; Sun., 2–5 p.m.). Small display of local material, replicas, fort-models and one distance slab.

Melrose Abbey Museum (Apr.–Sept: Mon.–Sat., 9.30 a.m.–7 p.m., Sun., 2–7 p.m; Oct.–Mar: Mon.–Sat., 9.30 a.m.–4 p.m; Sun., 2–4 p.m.). (Opening times subject to alteration.) Selection of finds from Newstead.

Selkirk Halliwell's House, Halliwell's Close (Apr.–Oct: Mon–Sat., 10 a.m.– 5 p.m; Sun., 2–5 p.m. Nov.–Dec: Mon.–Fri., 2–5 p.m.). Small display of local finds, including timber beam from Oakwood fort.

In addition, small collections of Roman material are held in several other museums, including Kilmarnock, Kirkintilloch, Perth, Hawick and Stirling. Though not permanently on view, Roman material there is included in temporary exhibitions from time to time.

Bibliography

Only a selection of the available general works can be noticed here, and for individual sites reference has been made only to major excavation reports and to the most recent discoveries, if any. Details of archaeological activity will be found in *Discovery and Excavation in Scotland*, published annually by the Council for British Archaeology Scotland (CBAS).

The Bibliography is subdivided according to the chapter headings used in the foregoing pages. For Part 2, the archaeological sites mentioned in each chapter are listed alphabetically except that the Gask Ridge watch-towers are considered as a single group. The letters and figures after each site-name are its National Grid Reference, which should ease their identification on OS maps.

Abbreviations used

DES	*Discovery & Excavation in Scotland*
GAJ	*Glasgow Archaeological Journal*
JRS	*Journal of Roman Studies*
PSAS	*Proceedings of the Society of Antiquaries of Scotland*
ROSWS	*The Roman Occupation of South-Western Scotland*, ed. S. N. Miller (Glasgow 1952)
TDGNHAS	*Transactions of the Dumfriesshire & Galloway Natural History & Antiquarian Society*
TGAS	*Transactions of the Glasgow Archaeological Society*
TRSNAW	*Topography of Roman Scotland North of the Antonine Wall*, O. G. S. Crawford (Cambridge 1949)

PART 1

Scotland on the eve of the Roman Invasion

G. and A. Ritchie, *Scotland: Archaeology and Early History* (London 1981)

A. L. F. Rivet (ed.), *The Iron Age in Northern Britain* (Edinburgh 1967)

I. A. Richmond (ed.), *Roman and Native in North Britain* (Edinburgh 1958)

B. W. Cunliffe, *Iron Age Communities in Britain* (London 1978)

G. S. Maxwell, 'Casus Belli: Native Pressures and Roman Policy', in L. Thoms (ed.), *The Romans in Scotland = Scottish Archaeological Forum* 7, 1975 (Edinburgh 1976), 31–50

L. Macinnes, 'Pattern and Purpose: the Settlement Evidence', in D. W. Harding (ed.), *Later Prehistoric Settlement* (Edinburgh 1982), 57–73

The Romans in Scotland: an Historical Outline

S. S. Frere, *Britannia* (London 1978)

J. Wacher, *Roman Britain* (London 1978)

M. Todd, *Roman Britain 55 BC – AD 400* (Brighton 1981)

P. Salway, *Roman Britain* (Oxford 1981)

L. Thoms (ed.), *The Romans in Scotland = Scottish Archaeological Forum* 7, 1975 (Edinburgh 1976)

J. Kenworthy (ed.), *The Scottish Campaigns of Agricola = Scottish Archaeological Forum* 12, 1980 (Edinburgh 1981)

D. J. Breeze, *The Northern Frontiers of Roman Britain* (London 1982)

A. R. Burn, *Agricola and Roman Britain* (London 1953)

R. M. Ogilvie and I. A. Richmond, *Cornelii Taciti de vita Agricolae* (Oxford 1967)

W. S. Hanson, 'The first Roman occupation of Scotland', in W. S. Hanson and L. J. F. Keppie (eds.), *Roman Frontier Studies 1979* (Oxford 1980), 15–43

J. K. St. Joseph, 'The camp at Durno, Aberdeenshire, and the Site of Mons Graupius', *Britannia* 9 (1978), 271–87

J. G. F. Hind, 'Caledonia and its occupation under the Flavians', *PSAS* 113 (1983), 373–78

D. J. Breeze and B. Dobson, *Hadrian's Wall* (Harmondsworth 1978)

A. S. Robertson, *The Antonine Wall* (Glasgow 1979)

G. Macdonald, *The Roman Wall in Scotland* (Oxford 1934)

W. Hanson and G. Maxwell, *Rome's North West Frontier: the Antonine Wall* (Edinburgh 1983)

B. R. Hartley, 'The Roman Occupations of Scotland: the Evidence of Samian Ware', *Britannia* 3 (1972), 1–45

D. J. Breeze, 'Roman Scotland during the reign of Antoninus Pius', in W. S. Hanson and L. J. F. Keppie (eds.), *Roman Frontier Studies 1979* (Oxford 1980), 45–60

A. R. Birley, *Septimius Severus: The African Emperor* (London 1971)

J. C. Mann, 'The Northern Frontier after A.D. 369', *GAJ* 3 (1974), 34–42

The Roman Army

G. Webster, *The Roman Imperial Army* (London 1985)

L. Keppie, *The Making of the Roman Army* (London 1984)

P. A. Holder, *The Roman Army in Britain* (London 1982)

E. B. Birley, 'The Fate of the Ninth Legion', in R. M. Butler (ed.), *Soldier and Civilian in Roman Yorkshire* (Leicester 1971), 71–80

Roman Military Installations

D. J. Breeze, *Roman Forts in Britain* (Aylesbury 1983)

A. Johnson, *Roman Forts of the 1st and 2nd centuries AD in Britain and the German Provinces* (London 1983)

R. J. A. Wilson, *Roman Forts: an illustrated Introduction to the Garrison Posts of Roman Britain* (London 1980)

G. Webster, *The Roman Imperial Army* (London 1985)

R. Chevallier, *Roman Roads* (London 1976)

I. D. Margary, *Roman Roads in Britain* (London 1973)

G. S. Maxwell, 'The evidence from the Roman Period', in A. Fenton and G. Stell (eds.), *Loads and Roads in Scotland and Beyond* (Edinburgh 1984), 21–48

D. E. Johnston, *An Illustrated History of Roman Roads in Britain* (Bourne End 1979)

The Monuments in the Landscape

O. G. S. Crawford, *Topography of Roman Scotland North of the Antonine Wall* (Cambridge 1949)

S. N. Miller (ed.), *The Roman Occupation of South-Western Scotland* (Glasgow 1952)

Piecing Together the Roman Past

R. G. Collingwood and R. P. Wright, *The Roman Inscriptions of Britain*, Vol. 1 (Oxford 1965)

A. R. Burn, *The Romans in Britain: an Anthology of Inscriptions* (Oxford 1969)

L. Keppie, *Roman Distance Slabs from the Antonine Wall* (Glasgow 1979)

P. J. Casey, *Roman Coinage in Britain* (Princes Risborough 1980)

A. S. Robertson, 'The Romans in North Britain: The Coin Evidence', in H. Temporini and W. Haase (eds.), *Aufstieg und Niedergang der römischen Welt*, II.3 (Berlin–New York 1975), 364–426

A. S. Robertson, 'The Circulation of Roman Coins in North Britain: the evidence of Hoards and Site-finds from Scotland', in R. A. G. Carson and C. M. Kraay (eds.), *Scripta Nummaria Romana* (London 1978), 186–216

A. C. Anderson, *Interpreting Roman Pottery* (London 1984)

J. Liversidge, *Britain in the Roman Empire* (London 1968)

R. G. Collingwood and I. A. Richmond, *The Archaeology of Roman Britain* (London 1969)

J. M. C. Toynbee, *Art in Britain under the Romans* (Oxford 1964)

L. J. F. Keppie and B. J. Arnold, *Corpus of Roman Sculpture (Corpus Signorum Imperii Romani)*, Vol. 1, fasc. 4 *(Scotland)* (London 1984)

A. S. Robertson, 'Roman Finds from non-Roman Sites in Scotland', *Britannia* 1 (1970), 198–226

The Rediscovery of Roman Scotland

R. Sibbald, *Historical Inquiries* (London 1707)

A. Gordon, *Itinerarium Septentrionale* (London 1726)

J. Horsley, *Britannia Romana* (London 1732)

University of Glasgow, *Monumenta Romani Imperii* (Glasgow 1768)

W. Roy, *Military Antiquities of the Romans in Britain* (London 1793)

W. Maitland, *History and Antiquities of Scotland* (London 1757)

R. Stuart, *Caledonia Romana* (2nd ed., Edinburgh and London 1852)

Glasgow Archaeological Society, *The Antonine Wall Report* (Glasgow 1899)

I. G. Brown, *The Hobby-Horsical Antiquary* (Edinburgh 1981)

J. K. S. St. Joseph, 'Aerial Reconnaissance of Roman Scotland, 1939–75', *GAJ* 4 (1975), 1–28

S. S. Frere and J. K. S. St. Joseph, *Roman Britain from the Air* (Cambridge 1983)

D. R. Wilson, *Air Photo Interpretation for Archaeologists* (London 1982)

G. S. Maxwell (ed.), *The Impact of Aerial Reconnaissance on Archaeology* (London 1983)

Life on the Frontier

D. V. Clarke, D. J. Breeze and G. Mackay, *The Romans in Scotland* (Edinburgh 1980)

A. S. Robertson and M. E. Scott, *The Roman Collections in the Hunterian Museum* (Glasgow, n.d.)

A. K. Bowman and J. D. Thomas, *The Vindolanda Writing Tablets* (London 1983)

P. Salway, *The Frontier People of Roman Britain* (Cambridge 1965)

The Impact of Rome

H. H. Scullard, *Roman Britain: Outpost of the Empire* (London 1979)

J. Wacher, *The Coming of Rome* (London 1979)

R. Miket and C. Burgess (eds.), *Between and Beyond the Walls* (Edinburgh 1984)

PART 2

Ordnance Survey, *Map of Roman Britain*, 4th ed. (HMSO 1978)

Ordnance Survey, *Map of the Antonine Wall* (HMSO 1969)

D. J. Breeze, *Roman Scotland: a Guide to the Visible Remains* (Newcastle 1979)

R. J. A. Wilson, *A Guide to the Roman Remains in Britain*, 2nd ed. (London 1980)

Scotland South of the Antonine Wall

General (including roads): S. N. Miller (ed.), *The Roman Occupation of South-Western Scotland* (Glasgow 1952) – hereafter *ROSWS*; R. C. Bruce, *Handbook to the Roman Wall* (rev. ed. C. M. Daniels) (Newcastle 1979); Royal Commission on the Ancient and Historical Monuments of Scotland (RCAHMS), Inventories: *Dumfriesshire* (Edinburgh 1920), *Midlothian and West Lothian* (Edinburgh 1929), *Peeblesshire* (Edinburgh 1967), *Selkirkshire* (Edinburgh 1957), *Roxburghshire* (Edinburgh 1956)

Bankhead (NS 971449) *Britannia* 15 (1984), 265

Barburgh Mill (NX 902884) D. J. Breeze, *Britannia* 5 (1974), 130–62

Barochan (NS 413690) F. Newall and A. Halifax Crawford, *DES* 1972, 35–36; L. J. F. Keppie and F. Newall, *DES* 1984, 34, 1985, 49

Beattock Summit (NS 999153) G. S. Maxwell, *Britannia* 7 (1976), 33–38

Birrens (NY 219752) A. S. Robertson, *Birrens (Blatobulgium)* (Edinburgh 1975)

Bishopton (NS 418720) K. A. Steer, *PSAS* 83 (1948–49), 28–32; *JRS* 40 (1950),93–94, 43 (1953),105–6, 44 (1954),86, 45 (1955),123

Bothwellhaugh (NS 731577) RCAHMS, *Lanarkshire*, 119–21; L. J. F. Keppie, *GAJ* 8 (1981), 46–94

Broomholm (NY 378814) R. W. Feachem, *TDGNHAS* 28 (1949–50), 188–89; *JRS* 52 (1962),164, 53 (1963),128, 55 (1965),202

Brownhart Law (NT 790096) J. K. St. Joseph, *PSAS* 83 (1948–49), 170–74; RCAHMS, *Roxburghshire*, 378–79

Burnswark (NY 186787) D. Christison, J. Barbour, J. Anderson, *PSAS* 33 (1898–99), 198–249; G. Jobey, *TDGNHAS* 53 (1977–78), 57–104

Cappuck (NT 695212) I. A. Richmond, *PSAS* 85 (1950–51), 138–45; RCAHMS, *Roxburghshire*, 381–83

Carzield (NX 968818) E. Birley and I. A. Richmond, *TDGNHAS*

22 (1938–39), 156–63; E. Birley and J. P. Gillam, *ibid*. 24 (1945–46), 69–78; *DES* 1956, 14

Castledykes (NS 929442) A. S. Robertson, *The Roman Fort at Castledykes* (Edinburgh 1964); RCAHMS, *Lanarkshire*, 124–28; E. Archer, *DES* 1984, 26

Castle Greg (NT 050592) RCAHMS, *Midlothian and West Lothian*, 140

Channelkirk (NT 473548) J. K. St. Joseph, *JRS* 51 (1961), 121

Chew Green (NT 788084) I. A. Richmond and G. S. Keeney, *Archaeologia Aeliana* ser. 4, 14 (1937), 129–50; I. A. Richmond, 'The Romans in Redesdale', *Northumberland County History* 15 (Newcastle 1940), 63–159

Cleghorn (NS 910459) RCAHMS, *Lanarkshire*, 128

Craik Cross (NT 303047) I. A. Richmond, *PSAS* 80 (1945–46), 103–17; J. K. St. Joseph, *TDGNHAS* 24 (1945–46), 151; RCAHMS, *Roxburghshire*, 402–3

Cramond (NT 189768) A. and V. Rae, *Britannia* 5 (1974), 163–224; frequent reports of more recent work in *DES*

Crawford (NS 953214) G. Maxwell, *PSAS* 104 (1971–72), 147–200; RCAHMS, *Lanarkshire*, 128–33

Dalmakethar (NY 107924) S. N. Miller, *ROSWS*, 101–3

Dalswinton (NX 933848) I. A. Richmond and J. K. St. Joseph, *TDGNHAS* 34 (1955–56), 9–21; E. Birley, *ibid.*, 35 (1956–57), 9–13

Drumlanrig (NX 854989) *Britannia* 16 (1985), 267.

Durisdeer (NS 902048) S. N. Miller, *ROSWS*, 124–26

Easter Happrew (NT 196401) K. A. Steer, *PSAS* 90 (1956–57), 93–101; RCAHMS, *Peeblesshire*, 169–71

Easter Langlee (NT 520361) K. A. Steer, *PSAS* 98 (1964–66), 320–21

Eildon Hill (NT 554328) RCAHMS, *Roxburghshire*, 306–10

Elginhaugh (NT 321673) G. S. Maxwell, *Britannia* 14 (1983), 167–81; *idem*, *DES* 1984, 18

Gatehouse of Fleet (NX 595575) J. K. St. Joseph, in B. R. Hartley and J. Wacher (eds.), *Rome and her Northern Provinces* (Gloucester 1983), 222–34

Gilnockie (NY 389792) RCAHMS, *Dumfriesshire*, 27–28

Girvan (NX 191991) J. K. St. Joseph, *Britannia* 9 (1978), 397–400

Glenlochar (NX 735645) I. A. Richmond and J. K. St. Joseph, *TDGNHAS* 30 (1951–52), 1–16

Inveresk (NT 342720) I. A. Richmond, *PSAS* 110 (1978–80), 286–

304; G. Thomas, *DES* 1977, 22; W. S. Hanson, *PSAS* 114 (1984), 251–59

Lamington (NS 977309) RCAHMS, *Lanarkshire*, 160

Lantonside (NY 010662) *Britannia* 16 (1985), 267

Little Clyde (NS 994159) RCAHMS, *Lanarkshire*, 134–35

Loudoun Hill (NS 605371) S. N. Miller, *ROSWS*, 188–91; D. L. Kennedy, *Britannia* 7 (1976), 286–87

Lurg Moor (NS 295737) *JRS* 43 (1953), 105; A. S. Robertson, *PSAS* 97 (1963–64), 198–200

Lyne (NT 187405) K. A. Steer and R. W. Feachem, *PSAS* 95 (1961–62), 208–18; RCAHMS, *Peeblesshire*, 171–75

Milton (NT 092014) J. Clarke, *TDGNHAS* 28 (1949–50), 199–221

Mollins (NS 713718) W. S. Hanson and G. S. Maxwell, *Britannia* 11 (1980), 43–49

Newstead (NT 571343) J. Curle, *A Roman Frontier Post and its People: the Fort of Newstead* (Glasgow 1911); RCAHMS, *Roxburghshire*, 312–20

Oakwood (NT 425249) K. A. Steer and R. W. Feachem, *PSAS* 86 (1951–52), 81–105; RCAHMS, *Selkirkshire*, 99–102

Outerwards (NS 232666) F. Newall, *GAJ* 4 (1976), 111–23

Pennymuir (NT 755140) RCAHMS, *Roxburghshire*, 375–77

Raeburnfoot (NY 251990) A. S. Robertson, *TDGNHAS* 29 (1960–61), 24–29

Redshaw Burn (NT 030139) S. N. Miller, *ROSWS*, 111; RCAHMS, *Lanarkshire*, 134–5

Rubers Law (NT 580156) RCAHMS, *Roxburghshire*, 102–5

Sanquhar (NS 785106) *Britannia* 16 (1985), 267

Torwood (NY 122819) S. N. Miller, *ROSWS*, 101

Wandel (NS 944268) RCAHMS, *Lanarkshire*, 136

Ward Law (NY 024668) S. N. Miller, *ROSWS*, 117–20; A. Truckell, *TDGNHAS* 27 (1948–49), 203

White Type (NT 055119) S. N. Miller, *ROSWS*, 24

Woden Law (NT 767125) RCAHMS, *Roxburghshire*, 169–72; I. A. Richmond and J. K. St. Joseph, *PSAS* 112 (1982), 277–84

The Antonine Wall

General: G. Macdonald, *The Roman Wall in Scotland* (Oxford 1934); A. S. Robertson, *The Antonine Wall* (Glasgow 1979); W.

Hanson and G. Maxwell, *Rome's North West Frontier: the Antonine Wall* (Edinburgh 1983); D. J. Breeze, *The Antonine Wall* (HMSO forthcoming); L. Keppie, 'The Antonine Wall 1960–1980', *Britannia* 13 (1982), 91–111; D. Skinner, *The Countryside of the Antonine Wall* (Perth 1973); K. A. Steer, 'The Nature and Purpose of the Expansions on the Antonine Wall', *PSAS* 90 (1956–57), 161–69; RCAHMS, Inventories: *Stirlingshire* (Edinburgh 1963); *Lanarkshire* (Edinburgh 1978)

Auchendavy (NS 677749) L. J. F. Keppie and J. J. Walker, *Britannia* 16 (1985), 29–35

Balmuildy (NS 581716) S. N. Miller, *The Roman Fort at Balmuildy* (Glasgow 1922)

Bar Hill (NS 707759) G. Macdonald and A. Park, *The Roman Forts on the Bar Hill* (Glasgow 1906); A. Robertson, M. Scott and L. Keppie, *Bar Hill, a Roman Fort and its Finds* (Oxford 1975); L. J. F. Keppie, *GAJ* 12 (1985), forthcoming

Bearsden (NS 545720) D. J. Breeze, 'The Roman Fort on the Antonine Wall at Bearsden', in D. J. Breeze (ed.), *Studies in Scottish Antiquity* (Edinburgh 1984), 32–68; *idem, The Roman Fort at Bearsden*, forthcoming

Buchley enclosure (NS 595720) W. S. Hanson and G. S. Maxwell, *Britannia* 14 (1983), 227–43

Cadder (NS 616725) J. Clarke, *The Roman Fort at Cadder* (Glasgow 1933)

Carriden (NT 025807) J. K. St. Joseph, *PSAS* 83 (1948–49), 167–74; I. A. Richmond and K. A. Steer, *PSAS* 90 (1956–57), 1–7

Castlecary (NS 790783) D. Christison and M. Buchanan, *PSAS* 37 (1902–3), 271–346; RCAHMS, *Stirlingshire*, 103–6

Castlehill (NS 525727) L. J. F. Keppie, *GAJ* 7 (1980), 80–84

Cleddans (NS 508723) L. J. F. Keppie and J. J. Walker, *Britannia* 12 (1981), 143–62

Croy Hill (NS 733765) G. Macdonald, *PSAS* 59 (1924–25), 288–90; *ibid.* 66 (1931–32), 243–76; *ibid.* 71 (1936–37), 32–71; W. S. Hanson and L. Keppie, *Current Archaeology* 62 (June 1978), 91–94; W. S. Hanson, in J. Fitz (ed.), *Limes: Akten des XI internationalen Limeskongresses* (Budapest 1977), 1–9

Duntocher (NS 495726) A. S. Robertson, *An Antonine Fort, Golden Hill, Duntocher* (Edinburgh and London 1957)

Falkirk (NS 886798) RCAHMS, *Stirlingshire*, 99; D. J. Breeze, *PSAS* 106 (1974–75), 200–3; L. J. F. Keppie and J. F. Murray, *PSAS* 111 (1981), 248–62

Glasgow Bridge (NS 636731) RCAHMS, *Lanarkshire*, 134

Inveravon (NS 951796) A. S. Robertson, *GAJ* 1 (1969), 37–42

Kinneil (NS 977803) L. J. F. Keppie and J. J. Walker, *Britannia* 12 (1981), 143–62; L. Keppie, *Britannia* 13 (1982), 97

Kirkintilloch (NS 651739) A. S. Robertson, *PSAS* 97 (1963–64), 180–88

Mumrills (NS 918794) G. Macdonald and A. O. Curle, *PSAS* 63 (1928–29), 396–575; K. A. Steer, *PSAS* 94 (1960–61), 86–132; RCAHMS, *Stirlingshire*, 96–99

Old Kilpatrick (NS 460731) S. N. Miller, *The Roman Fort at Old Kilpatrick* (Glasgow 1928)

Rough Castle (NS 843798) M. Buchanan, D. Christison, J. Anderson, *PSAS* 39 (1904–5), 442–99; RCAHMS, *Stirlingshire*, 100–2; I. MacIvor, M. C. Thomas and D. J. Breeze, *PSAS* 110 (1978–80), 230–85

Seabegs Wood (NS 812792) L. J. F. Keppie and J. J. Walker, *Britannia* 12 (1981), 143–62

Summerston (NS 578722) *Britannia* 12 (1981), 320

Watling Lodge (NS 862797) D. J. Breeze, *PSAS* 105 (1972–74), 166–75

Westerwood (NS 760773) G. Macdonald, *PSAS* 67 (1932–33), 243–96; L. J. F. Keppie, *GAJ* 5 (1979), 9–18

Wilderness Plantation (NS 597721) J. J. Wilkes, *GAJ* 3 (1974), 51–65; RCAHMS, *Lanarkshire*, 136–7

Scotland North of the Antonine Wall

General (including roads): O. G. S. Crawford, *Topography of Roman Scotland North of the Antonine Wall* (*TRSNAW*) (Cambridge 1949); RCAHMS, Inventory: *Stirlingshire* (Edinburgh 1963)

Abernethy (NO 174165) J. K. St. Joseph, *JRS* 63 (1973), 219–20

Ardoch (NN 839099) D. Christison, J. H. Cunningham, J. Anderson, T. Ross, *PSAS* 32 (1897–98), 399–476; J. K. St. Joseph, *Britannia* 1 (1970), 163–78; *idem*, *JRS* 67 (1977), 135–38; D. J. Breeze, in A. O'Connor and D. V. Clarke (eds.), *From the Stone Age to the 'Forty-five* (Edinburgh 1983), 224–36

Arthur's O'on (NS 879827) K. A. Steer, *Arch. J.* 115 (1958), 99–110; RCAHMS, *Stirlingshire*, 118; I. G. Brown, *Antiquity* 48 (1974), 283–87

Auchinhove (NJ 463517) J. K. St. Joseph, *JRS* 63 (1973), 227–28

Balmakewan (NO 665666) J. K. St. Joseph, *JRS* 59 (1969), 112

Bellie (NJ 355613) O. G. S. Crawford, *TRSNAW* 122–25; J. K. St. Joseph, *JRS* 59 (1969), 113–14; G. D. B. Jones and I Keillor, *DES* 1984, 12

Bertha (NO 097268) O. G. S. Crawford, *TRSNAW*, 56–62

Black Hill (NO 176391) I. A. Richmond, *PSAS* 74 (1939–40), 37–40

Bochastle (NN 614079) W. A. Anderson, *TGAS* n.s. 14 (1956), 35–63; J. K. St. Joseph, *JRS* 63 (1973), 224

Burnfield (NJ 540476) *Britannia* 15 (1984), 273

Camelon (NS 863809) D. Christison, M. Buchanan, J. Anderson, *PSAS* 35 (1900–01), 329–417; RCAHMS, *Stirlingshire*, 107–12; D. J. Breeze, J. Close-Brooks and J. N. G. Ritchie, *Britannia* 7 (1976), 73–95; N. McCord and J. Tait, *PSAS* 109 (1977–78), 151–65; V. A. Maxfield, *Scottish Archaeological Forum* 12 (1980), 69–78

Cardean (NO 289460) A. S. Robertson, in D. Haupt and H. G. Horn (eds.), *Studien zu den Militärgrenzen Roms* II (Köln/Bonn 1977), 65–74

Cargill (NO 163376 and NO 166379) I. A. Richmond, *JRS* 33 (1943), 47; J. K. St. Joseph and G. S. Maxwell, *Britannia* (forthcoming)

Carpow (NO 208179) R. E. Birley, *PSAS* 96 (1962–63), 184–207; J. K. St. Joseph, *JRS* 63 (1973), 220–23

Cleaven Dyke (NO 156408–171399) I. A. Richmond, *PSAS* 74 (1939–40), 37–48; H. C. Adamson, *DES* 1975, 42

Dalginross (NN 773210) O. G. S. Crawford, *TRSNAW*, 41–44; A. S. Robertson, *PSAS* 97 (1963–64), 196–98; J. K. St. Joseph, *JRS* 59 (1969), 109

Doune (NN 727012) G. S. Maxwell, *Britannia* 15 (1984), 217–23

Dunning (NO 025148) J. K. St. Joseph, *JRS* 63 (1973), 218–19

Drumquhassle (NS 484874) G. S. Maxwell, *Britannia* 14 (1983), 167–81

Durno (NJ 699272) J. K. St. Joseph, *JRS* 67 (1977), 141–42; *idem*, *Britannia* 9 (1978), 271–88

Fendoch (NN 919283) I. A. Richmond and J. McIntyre, *PSAS* 73 (1938–39), 110–54

Gask Ridge (NN 917185 to NO 020205) D. Christison, *PSAS* 35 (1900–1), 15–43; A. S. Robertson, in *Trans. Perthshire Soc. of Natural Sciences* 1974, 14–29

Glenbank (NN 812057) G. S. Maxwell, *DES* 1984, 4

Glenmailen (NJ 655381) G. Macdonald *PSAS* 50 (1915–16), 348–59; J. K. St. Joseph, *Britannia* 1 (1970), 163–78; *idem*, *JRS* 63 (1973), 226

Gourdie (NO 115427) I. A. Richmond, *JRS* 33 (1943), 47; O. G. S. Crawford, *TRSNAW*, 75–76

Grassy Walls (NO 105280) O. G. S. Crawford, *TRSNAW*, 64–67; J. K. St. Joseph, *JRS* 48 (1958), 91

Inchtuthil (NO 125397) J. Abercromby, T. Ross, J. Anderson, *PSAS* 36 (1901–02), 182–242; L. Pitts and J. K. St. Joseph, *Inchtuthil, the Roman Legionary Fortress* (London 1985)

Innerpeffray (NN 916182 and 907182) J. K. St. Joseph, *JRS* 48 (1958), 90; *ibid.* 59 (1969), 116

Inverquharity (NO 404582) G. S. Maxwell, *DES* 1983, 32; *Britannia* 15 (1984), 274; *DES* 1984, 35

Kaims Castle (NN 860129) D. Christison, *PSAS* 35 (1900–01), 15–43

Kair House (NO 767765) J. K. St. Joseph, *JRS* 55 (1965), 83; *idem*, *JRS* 63 (1973), 233

Kintore (NJ 787162) O. G. S. Crawford, *TRSNAW*, 112–15; J. K. St. Joseph, *JRS* 67 (1977), 140; A. N. Shepherd, *DES* 1984, 11–12

Kirkbuddo (NO 491442) O. G. S. Crawford, *TRSNAW*, 97–100; J. K. St. Joseph, *JRS* 48 (1958), 92–94; *ibid.* 55 (1965), 83

Lintrose (NO 220376) O. G. S. Crawford, *TRSNAW*, 84–86; J. K. St. Joseph, *JRS* 45 (1955), 87

Malling (NN 564000) J. K. St. Joseph, *JRS* 63 (1973), 223–24

Muiryfold (NJ 489520) J. K. St. Joseph, *JRS* 51 (1961), 123; *ibid* 59 (1969), 118

Normandykes (NO 829993) O. G. S. Crawford, *TRSNAW*, 110–12

Raedykes (NO 841902) G. Macdonald, *PSAS* 50 (1915–16), 317–48; J. K. St. Joseph, *JRS* 59 (1969), 118

Scone (NO 104270) J. K. St. Joseph, *JRS* 48 (1958), 92–94; *idem*, *JRS* 55 (1965), 83

Stracathro (NO 617657) J. K. St. Joseph, *Britannia* 1 (1970), 163–78; A. S. Robertson, in D. Haupt and H. G. Horn (eds.), *Studien zu den Militärgrenzen Roms* II (Köln/Bonn 1977), 65–74

Strageath (NN 898180) O. G. S. Crawford, *TRSNAW*, 40-41; annual reports of excavation work by S. S. Frere in *DES* from 1973 to 1980, and subsequently by J. J. Wilkes in *Britannia*

Index